Impairment of fixed assets and goodwill

A commentary on FRS 11

Impairment of fixed assets and goodwill

A commentary on FRS 11

By Hans Nailor, FCA
of PricewaterhouseCoopers, Chartered Accountants
London, March 1999

Published by:

Gee Publishing Limited
100 Avenue Road
Swiss Cottage
London
NW3 3PG
Tel: +44 (171) 393 7400
Fax:+44 (171) 393 7463
Website: www.gee.co.uk

This book aims to provide general guidance only and does not purport to deal with all the possible questions and issues that may arise in any given situation. Should the reader encounter particular problems he is advised to seek professional advice, which PricewaterhouseCoopers would be pleased to provide.

No responsibility for loss occasioned to any person acting or refraining from action as a result of any material in this publication can be accepted by the author or publisher.

Appendix 1 is reproduced with the permission of the Accounting Standards Board Limited.

PricewaterhouseCoopers is authorised by the Institute of Chartered Accountants in England and Wales to carry on investment business.

ISBN 186089 041 5

© PricewaterhouseCoopers, UK

Printed and bound in Great Britain by The Bath Press, Bath

Acknowledgement

The author acknowledges with thanks the assistance given by Jyoti Ghosh, Eddie Hodgson, Peter Holgate, Barry Johnson and Ian Wright, in the preparation of this text.

Thanks also to Barbara Willis and Amber Rollinson for their help in the production of the text.

March 1999

Contents

Contents

Chapter 1

Executive summary

1.1   FRS 11, 'Impairment of fixed assets and goodwill', applies to most categories of tangible and intangible fixed assets and to purchased goodwill that is treated as an asset. FRS 11 requires entities to focus more attention on their carrying values than previously.

1.2   The principles underlying the standard are not new. Long-established rules in the Companies Act and previous accounting standards restricted the balance sheet carrying values of fixed assets to their recoverable amounts. There was, however, little detailed guidance on how to calculate recoverable amounts of individual assets or, more generally, when diminution in values of assets should be regarded as permanent. FRS 11 puts in place a detailed methodology for identifying impairments and measuring recoverable amount. Thus its main impact is as a 'how to do it' standard.

1.3   FRS 11 does not require formal impairment reviews to be carried out annually. In general, the full rigours of the standard apply only when adverse economic conditions or other events indicate that assets might be impaired. However, there are rules in FRS 10, 'Goodwill and intangible assets' and in FRS 15, 'Tangible fixed assets' that require special impairment reviews of long-life assets, using FRS 11's methodology, to justify low or nil amortisation charges. The three standards operate to require impairment reviews in the following circumstances:

■   FRS 10 requires purchased goodwill and intangible assets to be reviewed for impairment at the end of each reporting period where the amortisation period is more than 20 years.

- FRS 15 requires tangible fixed assets (other than non-depreciable land) to be reviewed for impairment at the end of each reporting period when either no depreciation is charged on the grounds that it would be immaterial or when the asset's estimated remaining useful economic life is greater than 50 years.

- FRS 11 requires fixed assets and goodwill generally to be reviewed for impairment when there is an indicator of impairment.

1.4 FRS 11 requires greater use of cash flow projections to support asset values. The impairment tests are complex and assumptions about future cash flows are inherently subjective. Applying the standard in practice is as much art as science.

1.5 When an impairment review is required, the asset's recoverable amount should be estimated and compared with its carrying value. Recoverable amount is the higher of net realisable value and value in use. This reflects the greatest value of an asset in terms of the cash flows that can be derived from it, either by selling it or by continuing to use it in the business.

1.6 Cash flows are normally generated by groups of assets working together, rather than by individual fixed assets. If value in use cannot be estimated for individual assets, it should be estimated for groups of assets that generate income streams that are largely independent of each other. These are referred to as 'income-generating units'. Where an impairment review of an income-generating unit is required, it is intended to cover all its tangible assets, intangible assets and attributable goodwill.

1.7 In practice, dividing the activities of an enterprise into income-generating units is likely to be the first key step in carrying out impairment reviews. This establishes the level of aggregation at which impairment reviews should be carried out. Impairment reviews should as a matter of principle be carried out at the lowest level of aggregation that is practicable. Income-generating units should usually be identified in a way that is consistent with the way in which management makes decisions about continuing or closing different lines of business. Central assets and costs (such as corporate head offices or computer centres) that support the activities of income-generating units also need to be taken into account.

1.8 FRS 11 imposes a number of features to control the possibility of entities using over-optimistic forecasts to support asset values. These include disclosures where certain levels of longer term growth rates have been exceeded and requirements to monitor the accuracy of previous cash flow forecasts.

1.9 In general, impairment losses should be recognised within operating profit; there are special rules, however, relating to assets that have previously been revalued. In certain circumstances, impairment losses should be reversed, such as where recoverable amounts increase as a result of a change in economic conditions.

1.10 FRS 11 does not permit retrospective application. Any impairment losses identified when the standard is implemented for the first time should be charged in that year and not related back to an earlier year as a prior year adjustment.

1.11 FRS 11 was issued at the same time as the International Accounting Standards Committee published an accounting standard on the same subject, IAS 36 'Impairment of assets'. The requirements of FRS 11 and IAS 36 are very similar.

Executive summary

Chapter 2

Introduction

2.1 FRS 11, 'Impairment of fixed assets and goodwill', was published by the Accounting Standards Board (ASB) in July 1998 and applies to accounting periods ending on or after 23 December 1998.

2.2 The principles underlying the standard are not new. Long-established rules in the Companies Act and previous accounting standards (SSAP 12 'Accounting for depreciation') had the effect that the balance sheet carrying values of fixed assets should not exceed their recoverable amounts, that is, the net cash inflows they are expected to generate for the business. There was, however, little detailed guidance on how to apply those rules – for example, how cash flows could be related to individual assets, whether the cash flows should be measured on a discounted or undiscounted basis or, more generally, when a diminution in value should be regarded as permanent.

2.3 FRS 11 was issued at the same time as the International Accounting Standards Committee published an accounting standard on the same subject, IAS 36 'Impairment of assets'. The requirements of FRS 11 and IAS 36 are very similar.

2.4 FRS 11 evolved in conjunction with the development of the new methods of accounting for goodwill and intangible assets that are found in FRS 10, 'Goodwill and intangible assets', published by the ASB at the end of 1997 and which became effective at the same time as FRS 11. FRS 10 requires purchased goodwill to be treated as an asset and that both purchased goodwill and intangible assets should generally be amortised over a useful economic life not exceeding 20 years. However, FRS 10 also allows for the possibility that purchased goodwill and intangible assets can, in appropriate circumstances, be amortised over longer periods or be carried permanently on the balance sheet without amortisation (where the useful economic life is considered to be indefinite).

2.5 A key feature of FRS 10 is that impairment reviews must be performed in certain circumstances to check whether the carrying values of goodwill and intangibles are recoverable. If a company amortises goodwill or intangibles over more than 20 years or does not amortise them at all, it has to carry out an impairment review annually. An impairment review for long-life goodwill or intangible assets should be a rigorous exercise that would require an entity to demonstrate that, in respect of acquisitions, the present value of the incremental future cash flows was enough to justify the carrying value of the goodwill or intangible assets. Thus the detailed methodology relating to impairment reviews that is contained in FRS 11 evolved from the development of the goodwill standard.

2.6 FRS 11 requires entities to focus more attention on the carrying values of fixed assets than previously. Greater use is made of cash flow projections to support asset values. Less emphasis is placed on the distinction between permanent and temporary diminutions in value because, essentially, the standard is concerned with identifying diminutions in value that should be recognised immediately. The impairment tests are complex and assumptions about future cash flows are inherently subjective. Applying the standard in practice is as much art as science.

Transitional provisions

2.7 FRS 11 does not permit retrospective application. Any impairment losses identified when the standard is implemented for the first time should be charged in that year and not related back to an earlier year as a prior year adjustment. [FRS 11 para 75].

2.8 The ASB considers that FRS 11 is a refinement of existing accounting principles; thus any changes resulting from applying the standard for the first time should be treated as a change in estimate rather than as a change in accounting policy. This is notwithstanding the fact that an entity may previously have considered recoverable amount by assessing cash flows on a basis that was different from the methodology required by FRS 11, in particular by using undiscounted cash flows. Any previously unrecognised impairments that are identified by changing to FRS 11's discounted cash flow methodology must be charged in the year the standard is adopted, even though the underlying cause of the impairment may have occurred in a previous year.

Introduction

Chapter 3

Scope and objective of FRS 11

Scope of FRS 11

3.1   FRS 11 applies to purchased goodwill that is treated as an asset on the balance sheet and, with the following specific exceptions, to all tangible and intangible fixed assets. The exceptions, which are assets covered by other accounting pronouncements, are:

■   Fixed assets within the scope of FRS 13, 'Derivatives and other financial instruments: disclosures' – these include investments that are financial assets, such as investments in equity and non-equity shares and debt instruments.

   Investments in subsidiaries, quasi-subsidiaries, associates and joint ventures are, however, excluded from the scope of FRS 13 and thus in effect included in the scope of FRS 11.

■   Investment properties within the scope of SSAP 19.

■   Own shares held by an ESOP and shown as a fixed asset in the entity's balance sheet (under UITF 13 'Accounting for ESOP Trusts').

■   Costs relating to oil and gas exploration that have been capitalised pending the determination of whether or not economically developable reserves exist, which continue to be accounted for under the Oil Industry Accounting Committee's SORP 2, 'Accounting for oil and gas exploration and development activities'.
[FRS 11 para 5].

3.2 FRS 11 does not apply to current assets; neither does it apply to purchased goodwill that was previously written off to reserves and that remains so under the transitional arrangements of FRS 10.

Objective

3.3 FRS 11's objectives are to ensure that:

■ The carrying values of fixed assets and goodwill do not exceed their recoverable amount.

■ Impairment losses are recognised and measured on a consistent basis.

■ Adequate disclosures are given concerning the impact of impairment on an entity's financial position and performance. [FRS 11 para 1].

3.4 The principle that an asset's carrying value should not exceed its recoverable amount is already well established. What FRS 11 does, in order to set standards for recognition and measurement of impairment losses, is put in place a detailed methodology for identifying impairments and measuring recoverable amount where none existed before. Thus its main impact is as a 'how to do it' standard.

3.5 Although the methodology is complex and recoverable amount calculations may appear to be precise and detailed, it needs to be borne in mind when applying the standard that the calculations are based on best estimates of unknown future events. The forecasts that may be required are inherently judgemental and subjective. If assets need to be written down to reflect impairment, the write-offs are likely in practice to reflect fairly broad estimates of material impairment losses. The impairment review is not a precise science. Hence, although companies should make realistic estimates, there is no need to aim for spurious accuracy in the calculations.

Chapter 4

Identifying assets that may be impaired

Definition of impairment

4.1 The basic principle is that a fixed asset may not be carried in the balance sheet at more than its recoverable amount. An impairment is defined in FRS 11 as *"a reduction in the recoverable amount of a fixed asset or goodwill below its carrying amount"*. [FRS 11 para 2].

4.2 An asset's recoverable amount represents its greatest value to the business in terms of the cash flows that it can generate. That is the higher of what the asset could be sold for, net of direct selling expenses, (net realisable value) and the cash flows that are expected to be generated from its continued use in the business, including those from its ultimate disposal (value in use). Value in use is explicitly based on present value calculations.

4.3 The theory is that this measurement basis reflects the economic decisions that management makes when assets become impaired – is the business better off disposing of the asset or keeping it in use? An asset is impaired only if both net realisable value and value in use are lower than its carrying value.

4.4 An impairment review involves estimating an asset's recoverable amount and comparing it with its carrying value, as illustrated in the panel below. If net realisable value cannot be estimated reliably (for example, if there is no active market in the asset), recoverable amount is determined by estimating value in use alone. If the recoverable amount is lower than the carrying value, the asset is impaired and must be written down to the recoverable amount. A write-off cannot be avoided by arguing that the diminution in value is not permanent.

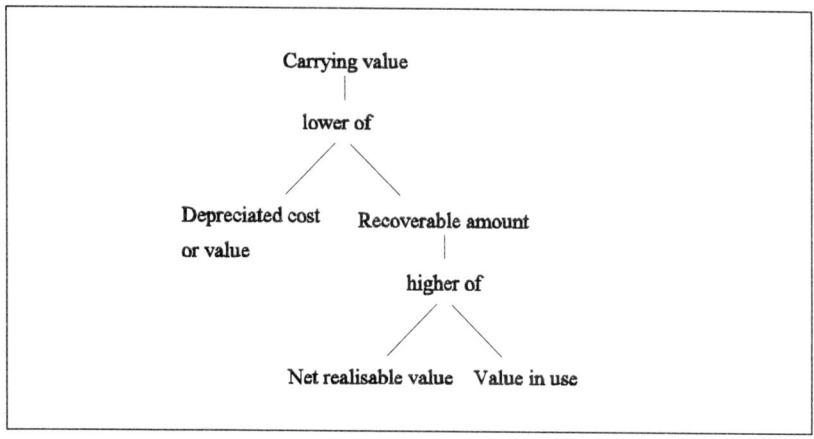

4.5 The standard is written from the perspective of commercial enterprises where fixed assets are employed to generate cash flows for the business. Where fixed assets are not held for the purpose of generating cash flows (such as certain assets held by non-profit making organisations), the value to such organisations of fixed assets acquired for the purpose of carrying out their activities cannot meaningfully be measured in terms of cash flow, because the benefits that derive from their use are not financial. Furthermore, such assets typically do not generate cash flows to cover financing costs or replacement. The normal accounting treatment for such assets is that they are depreciated systematically over their estimated useful lives, that is, as they wear out or as the benefits are otherwise consumed. The standard refers briefly to this issue and explains that it may not be appropriate to write down such assets to their recoverable amount and that "*an alternative measure of its service potential may be more relevant*". [FRS 11 para 20]. In practice, an impairment of an asset employed in a non-cash generating activity is likely to arise only where the asset suffers impairment in a physical sense, for example, where the asset is physically damaged or where the quality of service that it provides has deteriorated. As long as such assets continue to provide the anticipated benefits to the organisation, the consumption of such benefits will be reflected in regular depreciation charges.

Deferred tax taken into account

4.6   FRS 11 explains that in determining whether recoverable amount (and, hence, the measurement of any impairment losses) should be based on net realisable value or value in use, any deferred tax balances that would arise in each case should be taken into account. [FRS 11 para 19].

4.7   The value of an asset to the business is affected by tax considerations, such as future tax reliefs or capital gains tax liabilities, that would typically be taken into account when deciding whether the business is better off disposing of the asset or keeping it in use. Thus, if a disposal at market value would give rise to a capital gains tax liability, this should be 'netted off' the calculation of net realisable value when comparing it with value in use. However, although the comparison should be made on a 'net of tax' basis, the impaired carrying value of the asset (that is the estimated recoverable amount), whether it is based on net realisable value or value in use, should be recognised in the financial statements on a 'before tax' basis and any related deferred tax balances should be recognised separately as is normal practice. Similarly, any impairment losses should be recognised on a 'before tax' basis in the profit and loss account and the deferred tax effects are picked up in the tax line.

4.8   Comparing asset values net of deferred tax effects may be difficult to apply in practice within the existing 'partial provision' basis of deferred tax accounting required by SSAP 15. That is because deferred tax assets and liabilities tend to reflect the combined effect of timing differences rather than looking separately at each timing difference, such as that relating to an impaired asset. Thus, for example, in situations where no deferred tax is provided on an aggregate basis, there would be none to take into account when comparing net realisable value and value in use, if the tax situation is such that no tax would crystallise.

When impairment reviews are required

4.9 FRS 11 does not require formal impairment reviews to be carried out annually. In general, the full rigours of the standard apply only when there is an indication that assets might be impaired. If there are no such indications, there may be no reason to suspect that assets might be impaired.

4.10 However, there are special rules in FRS 10 and in FRS 15, 'Tangible fixed assets'. FRS 10 requires purchased goodwill and intangible assets to be reviewed for impairment at the end of each reporting period where the amortisation period is more than 20 years; it also requires a special first year impairment review of goodwill and intangible assets relating to new acquisitions (at the end of the first full year following the acquisition). FRS 15 requires tangible fixed assets (other than non-depreciable land) to be reviewed for impairment at the end of each reporting period when either no depreciation is charged on the grounds that it would be immaterial or when the asset's estimated remaining useful economic life is greater than 50 years. Where annual impairment reviews are required, they should be carried out in accordance with FRS 11.

4.11 Where fixed assets or goodwill are being depreciated over relatively short periods, depreciation reduces the risk of impairment, but where assets or goodwill have very long economic lives, the greater is the risk that they may become impaired in the future. FRS 11 states that for tangible fixed assets impairments will be an infrequent addition to depreciation, which is likely to be the case provided that depreciation rates and useful economic lives of assets are determined realistically and reviewed frequently.

Impairment indicators

4.12 FRS 11 requires that a review for impairment of a fixed asset or goodwill should be carried out if events or changes in circumstances indicate that the carrying amount of the fixed asset or goodwill may not be recoverable. [FRS 11 para 8].

4.13 FRS 11 includes a list of circumstances which may indicate that there has been an impairment. These are:

■   A current period operating loss in the business in which the fixed asset or goodwill is involved or net cash outflow from the operating activities of that business, combined with either past operating losses or net cash outflows from such operating activities or an expectation of continuing operating losses or net cash outflows from such operating activities.

■   A significant decline in a fixed asset's market value during the period.

■   Evidence of obsolescence or physical damage to the fixed asset.

■   A significant adverse change in:

 ■   Either the business or the market in which the fixed asset or goodwill is involved, such as the entrance of a major competitor.

 ■   The statutory or other regulatory environment in which the business operates.

 ■   Any 'indicator of value' (for example, turnover) used to measure the fair value of a fixed asset on acquisition.

■ A commitment by management to undertake a significant reorganisation.

■ A major loss of key employees.

■ A significant increase in market interest rates or other market rates of return that are likely to affect materially the fixed asset's recoverable amount.

[FRS 11 para 10].

4.14 The above list is not intended to be exhaustive and it is important not to ignore the obvious. Other indicators may be apparent that are relevant to the particular circumstances of a business. If there are any, an impairment review should be carried out. For example, a significant devaluation of the currency in which the business derives its cash flows may require the recoverable amount of its assets to be investigated. Or management's own forecasts may show a significant decline from previous budgets and forecasts. A decision to sell an under-performing business would also give rise to a review of its asset values if impairment losses had not been identified and recognised earlier.

4.15 Most of the examples of impairment indicators are self-explanatory. They reflect adverse events or conditions that affect either the assets directly or the business in which they are employed. They should normally trigger a review for impairment where they are relevant to the measurement of the fixed assets or goodwill.

4.16 Two of the items deserve particular comment. The first concerns increases in interest rates. Some may find it curious that, in historical cost accounting, an increase in interest rates should be an indicator of impairment. For example, if the expected operating cash flows are still healthy, why should there be a need to write down the assets? In present value terms, of course, the value of those operating cash flows is reduced if interest rates rise. The effect of calculating an asset's recoverable amount on the present value basis required by FRS 11 is that an asset will be deemed to be impaired unless it can earn sufficient to recover not only its carrying value but also its cost of capital. Therefore, if interest rates rise, the asset may need to earn more to recover a higher cost of capital. However, only significant movements in long-term rates would normally be relevant. FRS 11 emphasises that increases in short-term interest rates would not necessarily trigger an impairment review, because they may not affect the rate of return the market would require on long-term assets. [FRS 11 para 11].

4.17 The second item concerns a fall in an asset's market value. Net realisable value is only one part of the recoverable amount equation and some may question why the asset needs to be reviewed for impairment if there is no intention to sell it. However, since changes in market values reflect general economic conditions, it is reasonable that a significant fall in value should be worthy of further investigation (at least to consider whether it is relevant), as the asset's value to the business could have declined in a similar way to its value in the economy as a whole.

4.18 The equivalent International Accounting Standard (IAS 36) contains another indicator that is not mentioned in FRS 11. That is where the carrying value of the enterprise's net assets exceeds its market capitalisation. Where net asset value significantly exceeds market capitalisation for an extended period, this suggests that the market believes that the present value of the cash flows that the enterprise will earn is less than the aggregate carrying value of its net assets. This situation merits careful consideration and an impairment review may be appropriate. Either the market is more pessimistic about the company's future prospects than the company's management, in which case the management may wish to release further information, or the market is right and some assets are impaired.

4.19 There may, however, be several explanations for the situation where an entity's market capitalisation is less than its net asset value. One is that the entity may be in a cyclical business where stock market values tend to reflect short-term rather than long-term prospects and, hence, also show a history of market values falling for a period and then rising again. It is also notable that the instance of 'break-up' bids and demergers has often resulted in the 'sum of the parts' of an entity realising more value than the market capitalisation of the whole entity. Thus the fact that market capitalisation may sometimes be below net asset value is not always a conclusive indicator of impairment.

Special rules for goodwill and intangible assets

4.20 For goodwill and intangible fixed assets, the requirements for impairment reviews differ according to whether goodwill is amortised over more or less than 20 years, as illustrated below.

Impairment reviews	
Useful life 20 years or less	**Useful life more than 20 years**
End of first full year (simplified review)	Every year (detailed review)
Other years — high level check for impairment indicators — detailed review only if impairment indicators are present	

4.21 The requirements for impairment reviews are set out in FRS 10. Apart from the first year review (see below), the methodology for performing the reviews set out in FRS 11 should be followed.

4.22 A threshold of 20 years is specified in FRS 10, below which the impairment reviews are less onerous than for longer periods. Where goodwill or an intangible asset is written off over a shorter period, there is less risk of impairment, because its net book value diminishes more quickly.

4.23 A detailed impairment review of goodwill and intangible assets is required in the following situations:

- Where they are treated as having a useful life of more than 20 years, at the end of each reporting period (including the one in which the acquisition took place).

- Where their useful life is 20 years or less:

  - At the end of the first full year following their acquisition, *only* if there is an indicator of impairment or if the first year review (see below) indicates that the post-acquisition performance has failed to meet pre-acquisition expectations.

  - In other years, *only* if there is an indicator of impairment (that is, following the normal procedures for identifying fixed assets that may be impaired).

4.24 Where goodwill has to be reviewed annually for impairment, but is not actually expected to be impaired, the reviews in subsequent years after the first annual review can often be performed by updating the calculations performed for the first review. FRS 10 notes that if there have been no adverse changes since the first review, it may be possible to ascertain immediately that there has been no impairment. [FRS 10 para 38].

First year review

4.25 Where newly acquired goodwill or intangible assets are being amortised over 20 years or less, a first year impairment review is required. Purchased goodwill and most recognised intangible assets are acquired through business acquisitions. No equivalent review is required for newly acquired tangible fixed assets. This review should be carried out at the end of the first full financial year following their acquisition. It is intended to identify factors such as:

- Overpayment.
- Under-performance compared with expectations.

■ Material adverse changes to the acquired business in the immediate post-acquisition period.

4.26 The first year review has two stages. The first stage in effect requires management formally to consider whether the acquisition has lived up to expectations. This is done by comparing post-acquisition performance with the forecasts used in the acquisition appraisal and by considering whether there have been any other unexpected adverse events or changes in circumstances that throw doubt on the recoverability of the capitalised goodwill or intangible assets. For all acquisitions that give rise to significant amounts of purchased goodwill or intangible assets, the requirement for the first year review means that management needs to document formally the projections used at the time of the acquisition.

4.27 If the acquisition passes the first stage, there is no need to go on to the second stage. The second stage is a full impairment review, which is only required if the first test is failed or if there is any other indicator of impairment. [FRS 10 para 40].

Companies Act's requirements

4.28 The Companies Act's rules on impairments are framed in terms of 'permanent diminutions in value' and 'temporary diminutions in value'. There has often been difficulty in determining what is permanent and what is temporary. The Companies Act requires that a company must make provision if *any* fixed asset (including a fixed asset investment) has diminished in value, and this reduction is expected to be *permanent*. In such a situation, the company must reduce the amount at which it recognises the asset in its financial statements by the amount of this diminution in value. This requirement applies whether or not the asset has a limited useful economic life. [4 Sch 19(2)].

4.29 FRS 11 does not specifically use the term 'permanent diminution' or contrast this with a temporary diminution. Where an impairment is identified in accordance with the methodology of the standard, the asset should be written down. In the case of fixed assets carried on the historical cost basis, the tests in the standard are designed to identify impairments that should be regarded as permanent. Where assets are carried at revaluation, any impairment identified using the tests in the standard will still be regarded as a loss that must be recognised, but FRS 11 specifies that the presentation of the loss will vary according to whether the impairment arises from:

- a clear consumption of economic benefits; or

- other impairments, for example impairments arising from general changes in prices.

These presentation issues are considered in chapter 10.

4.30 FRS 11 also introduces the concept of the income-generating unit (IGU), which contrasts with the Act's requirements that *"...in determining the aggregate of any item the amount of each individual asset or liability that falls to be taken into account shall be determined separately"*. Whilst the Act, therefore, appears to require each asset or liability to be looked at separately, the standard requires assets and liabilities to be grouped together in some circumstances for the purpose of testing assets for impairment.

4.31 The standard, however, makes it clear that IGUs should be identified by dividing the total income of an entity into as many largely independent income steams as is reasonably practicable. Thus, it aims to ensure that the smallest possible grouping of income-earning assets and liabilities that is independent of the rest of the entity's income is chosen. This aims to come as close to the Act's requirements as is in practice possible, whilst at the same time being practical by recognising that assets that are inter-dependent can only be tested as one unit. Nonetheless, the standard emphasises that the value in use of a fixed asset should be estimated individually where reasonably practicable.

Identifying assets that may be impaired

Chapter 5

Measuring recoverable amount

General matters

5.1 FRS 11 defines recoverable amount as the higher of net realisable value and value in use. This reflects the greatest value of an asset in terms of the cash flows that can be derived from it, either by selling it or by continuing to use it in the business.

5.2 Both net realisable value and value in use can be difficult to determine in practice. FRS 11 recognises that disposal values cannot always be estimated – recoverable amount should then be determined by estimating value in use alone. As explained in subsequent chapters, estimating value in use is a matter of judgement, not fact, requiring estimates of cash flows many years into the future and determining appropriate discount rates to bring them back to their present values. The objective is to make estimates as realistic as possible.

5.3 It is not always necessary to calculate both measures when performing an impairment review. For instance, if net realisable value can be reliably estimated and is higher than the carrying amounts being reviewed, there is no need to calculate value in use. Similarly, if it is clear that net realisable value is lower than value in use, there is no need to calculate net realisable value.

5.4 In some circumstances it may be apparent from a quick review of financial data that the value in use of an asset will either exceed its carrying value or be exceeded by its net realisable value, in which case a detailed calculation of value in use is not required. [FRS 11 para 18]. For example, where goodwill has to be reviewed for impairment each year (because its useful life is greater than 20 years) and there was previously substantial leeway between the value in use and the carrying value, a simple check on actual performance against previous estimates may be sufficient to demonstrate that value in use continues to exceed carrying value.

5.5 Where an asset is to be disposed of, its net realisable value and value in use will generally be approximately the same, because value in use then reflects mainly the net cash proceeds expected from the asset's disposal.

Net realisable value

5.6 The definition of net realisable value is *"...the amount at which an asset could be disposed of, less any direct selling costs"*. [FRS 11 para 2].

5.7 In calculating net realisable value, direct selling costs are deducted. Such costs include, for instance, legal costs and stamp duty or perhaps costs of removing a sitting tenant before selling a building.

5.8 However, costs associated with reducing or reorganising the business, such as costs of making staff redundant, that may be incurred before a factory building could be sold should not be deducted in arriving at net realisable value (nor should any incremental income from changes in capacity be assumed). Those costs are not regarded as part of the costs of selling the asset itself. [FRS 11 para 23]. Provisions for certain reorganisation costs are recognised (as liabilities) when the criteria of FRS 12, 'Provisions, contingent liabilities and contingent assets', are met, that is, when the company has a constructive obligation to carry out the reorganisation. If there is no such obligation at the time the asset is being reviewed for impairment, no provision is made. Either way, the question of whether provisions for reorganisation costs should be made does not affect the calculation of the asset's net realisable value.

5.9 Net realisable value is based on market value where there is an active market. Whilst active markets may exist, for example, in second-hand cars, commercial vehicles, computer equipment, certain plant and machinery and many types of property, they may not exist for specialised plant or buildings. For those assets it may also be difficult to find recent transactions for similar assets to provide reliable evidence of potential sales proceeds.

5.10 Similarly, the net realisable value of an intangible asset may be difficult to determine, unless there is an active market from which a reliable market value can be derived, which is rare. In practice, unless a business is being sold, its goodwill is unlikely to have a net realisable value that can be determined directly.

5.11 Where an asset is in the process of being sold, the expected sale proceeds (less expected selling costs) may provide reliable evidence of net realisable value. Similarly, where a business is being sold, the expected sale proceeds may provide reliable evidence of the net realisable value of its recognised net assets and goodwill. For example, a binding sale contract entered into after the balance sheet date would provide the best evidence, but an intended sale where negotiations are in progress may in some cases also provide reliable evidence of net realisable value.

5.12 If net realisable value is found to be lower than the carrying amount of the asset, it should not automatically be written down to that value. For example, some assets could be sold only for their scrap value, because no market exists for the particular second-hand asset, and value in use may well be much higher. Before a write-down is booked, the asset's value in use also needs to be estimated in order to determine whether it is higher than its net realisable value. If it is, the impairment write-down, if any, is calculated by reference to value in use.

Value in use

5.13 The definition of value in use is *"the present value of the future cash flows obtainable as a result of an asset's continued use, including those resulting from its ultimate disposal".* [FRS 11 para 2].

5.14 Where reasonably practicable, the value in use of a fixed asset should be estimated individually.

5.15 Investments that are within the scope of FRS 11 – subsidiaries, associates and joint ventures – generate cash flows as discrete assets and should normally be considered individually. To be consistent with the way such entities are accounted for, their value in use should normally be based on the future net cash flows of the underlying entities that are attributable to the group's interest, rather than on the basis of dividend flows. For associates and joint ventures, the carrying value of the group's interest reflects two elements – the group's share of net assets and any purchased goodwill. Any impairments in the underlying fixed assets should already be picked up in the financial statements of the associate or joint venture.

5.16 Measuring the value in use of most fixed assets (tangible and intangible) is not straightforward, because they do not generate cash flows by themselves. Cash flows are normally generated by groups of assets working together, usually by the whole range of assets used in a business. Goodwill by definition is not a separable asset and always has to be considered as part of a group of assets in a business unit. Therefore, in practice a degree of aggregation is necessary in order to estimate value in use for complete groups of assets and associated goodwill.

5.17 If value in use cannot be estimated for individual assets, it should be estimated for groups of assets that generate income streams that are largely independent of each other. These are referred to as income-generating units (IGUs). Where an impairment review of an IGU is required, it is intended to cover all its tangible assets, intangible assets and attributable goodwill. The carrying value of each IGU containing the fixed asset or goodwill being reviewed should be compared with the higher of its value in use or net realisable value (if net realisable value can be measured reliably). If net realisable value cannot be measured reliably – which is frequently the case for IGUs – the recoverable amount of an IGU is determined by estimating its value in use alone.

5.18 In summary, the key steps in calculating value in use for groups of assets are:

■ Identifying separate IGUs.

■ Establishing carrying values for the net assets of each IGU, comprising the assets and liabilities attributable to the IGU, plus allocated goodwill.

■ Forecasting the future cash flows of the income-generating unit and discounting them to their present value.

■ Comparing the present value of the cash flows with the carrying amounts of the net assets attributable to the income-generating unit and recognising any shortfall as an impairment loss.

The details of the methodology and calculations are considered in the following chapters.

5.19 When considering impairment issues, the separate valuation principles and the objective of FRS 11 (that fixed assets should be recorded in the financial statements at no more than their recoverable amount) should always be borne in mind. For example, if an individual asset is clearly no longer providing service potential (say, as a result of physical damage) it obviously has a recoverable amount of zero (or scrap value) and should be written off immediately, irrespective of whether the cash flows of the income-generating unit are sufficient to recover the carrying value of all its assets, including the one that has become redundant.

Chapter 6

Income-generating units

Identifying income-generating units

6.1   In most practical situations, dividing the activities of an enterprise into IGUs is the first key step in carrying out impairment reviews. This establishes the level of aggregation at which impairment reviews should be carried out.

6.2   In general, the higher the level of aggregation the greater is the risk that impairment losses on unprofitable assets might be masked by unrecognised increases in value of profitable ones. Hence, impairment reviews should as a matter of principle be carried out at the lowest level that is practicable.

6.3   FRS 11 indicates that IGUs can be aggregated (that is, groups of similar IGUs can be considered as one IGU) for the purpose of determining value in use, provided that the level of aggregation is reasonable in the circumstances of the impairment review and that material impairments would not escape recognition by such aggregation. The rationale is that the standard is only concerned with identifying material impairments. [FRS 11 para 26]. Aggregation has important practical implications for businesses (such as retailers) that trade through a large number of separate outlets, since it may be impracticable, or at least costly, for businesses to prepare separate cash flow forecasts for large numbers of individual outlets.

6.4   An income-generating unit is defined as:

> *"A group of assets, liabilities and associated goodwill that generates income that is largely independent of the*

reporting entity's other income streams. The assets and liabilities include those directly involved in generating the income and an appropriate portion of those used to generate more than one income stream". [FRS 11 para 2].

6.5 IGUs should be identified *"by dividing the total income of the business into as many largely independent income streams as is reasonably practicable in the light of the information available to management"*. [FRS 11 para 28].

6.6 An asset or business that is to be disposed of forms an IGU of its own and does not belong to any other IGU. [FRS 11 para 31]. Its recoverable amount consists mainly of the expected net proceeds from disposal and these are independent of the income streams of other assets or businesses.

6.7 For continuing operations, management has discretion to identify IGUs to fit their information systems within the following parameters set out in FRS 11:

■ The groups of assets and liabilities should be as small as is reasonably practicable (consistent with the principle that assets should be valued separately).

■ The income streams of each IGU should be largely independent of each other and should be capable of being monitored separately.

■ IGUs are likely to be identified in a way that is consistent with the way in which management makes decisions about continuing or closing different lines of business.

■ IGUs may be identified by reference to major products or services.

■ Unique intangible assets (such as brands and mastheads) can often be used to identify IGUs, because they may generate income independently of each other and are usually monitored separately. [FRS 11 paras 27 to 29].

6.8 Several commentators on FRED 15 (the exposure draft that preceded FRS 11) referred to the subjectivity involved in identifying IGUs and raised issues as to when income streams are really independent. For example, in businesses that operate large numbers of retail outlets, such as stores, restaurants and financial services, different companies may take different views as to whether an IGU is an individual retail outlet or a group of outlets in a smaller or larger geographical region. Activities can also be cut in different ways – by geographical areas, product lines or in some other way. Much depends on how the operations are managed and how independent or interdependent they are.

6.9 In response to respondents' concerns about this issue, additional guidance was introduced into the FRS in the form of four mini-case studies. Although these are helpful, selection of IGUs remains a very judgmental area, particularly for vertically integrated operations and for businesses with multi-locations in retailing or manufacturing.

6.10 The first example in the FRS is a transport company operating a trunk route fed by supporting routes, which should be combined for the purposes of determining an IGU. The reasons given are that the cash flows of each route are not independent and that economic decisions about continuing or closing the supporting routes are not based on their returns in isolation.

6.11 An analogous situation is where a public transport operator runs a number of unprofitable routes in order to have access to profitable ones – it could not obtain the benefits of the latter without incurring the cost of the former where it may be under contract to provide a specified minimum level of service. Each route may or may not have its own dedicated assets and identifiable revenues and operating costs, but the income of each route is not independent in an economic sense, because management could not decide to discontinue any one route. The IGU for the assets of each route may be the whole franchise.

6.12 The second example in the FRS is a manufacturer that can allocate production across a number of facilities. One facility may be operating with surplus capacity and, hence, might be considered to be impaired if it were reviewed in isolation. However, there is not enough surplus capacity overall to enable any one manufacturing site to be closed. The FRS explains that, in this situation, the IGU should comprise all the sites at which the product can be made, because the cash inflows generated by any one site depend on the allocation of production across all sites. Therefore, the facilities are not reviewed separately, because impairment indicators affect them all together – at the larger IGU level, there may be no impairment.

Retail establishments

6.13 The third example in the FRS is a restaurant chain. The example concludes that each restaurant is a separate IGU, because its income is independent of the income of other restaurants – the cash inflows of each restaurant can be individually monitored and sensible allocations of costs to each restaurant can be made. However, since any impairment of individual restaurants is unlikely to be material, groups of restaurants that are affected by the same economic factors may be reviewed for impairment together for the purpose of identifying material impairments.

6.14 This example is relevant to a large spectrum of retail establishments but, in general, is of limited use in helping to reach a clear-cut view on whether an IGU is an individual site, a group of sites in a region, a country or the whole business. For the majority of modern multi-site retailers some level of aggregation of sites is normally appropriate. Whether a larger grouping is treated as an IGU or whether each site is taken to be an IGU, but a pragmatic view of aggregation is taken on grounds of materiality, as in the restaurant example referred to above.

Apart from other considerations, in some circumstances it may be impractical (or at least costly) to prepare detailed cash flow forecasts for each individual site – in any case, forecasts may to some extent be based on macro-assumptions about factors that affect larger groupings in a similar way. Some further examples are discussed below.

6.15 Judging which grouping of outlets produces largely independent income streams requires the characteristics of the way the business is managed to be assessed, for example, by considering whether:

■ Performance is monitored at individual, regional or other levels – for example, considering the lowest level at which meaningful profitability statements are produced.

■ Product offering and investment decisions are made at individual, regional or other grouping levels.

■ Individual outlets generate custom for other parts of the network.

■ Units are managed on a combined basis sharing systems, centralised purchasing and distribution functions.

■ Product pricing is determined locally or on an area or national basis.

6.16 Where regional or other groupings of establishments are taken as the normal basis for carrying out impairment reviews, any specific indicators of impairment affecting a smaller grouping would also need to be taken into account to ensure that material impairments are properly identified. Examples might include the entry of a major competitor into a local area, or the closure of a town's principal employer, both of which could have a long-term effect on the income of establishments in that area. A specific review of the smaller grouping or individual establishment affected by a local impairment indicator would then be necessary.

Banks and building society branches

6.17 Banking and building society branches generally sell a variety of products that are supported by central operations. In many ways the outlets represent a conduit for the central organisation which determines product pricing on a national basis. Whilst it may be possible to look at the income of each branch as being separate from the others, it is likely that very broad assumptions would need to be made to arrive at a measure of profitability, particularly in respect of recurring products such as life policies and savings schemes. In these circumstances it is unlikely that a branch is an IGU, unless for some reason management addresses profitability or contribution at a branch level. It is also unlikely that an individual branch would be material to the organisation.

Public houses

6.18 The income of individual pubs would usually be largely independent of others, and their performance would be capable of being monitored separately. Thus in the main they would be individual IGUs. However, as with the restaurants example in the FRS, where large numbers are operated it is unlikely that any one pub would be material and so it may be acceptable to consider them in groupings affected by the same economic factors.

Hotels

6.19 Individual hotels would usually generate income that is largely independent of others and their performance would be monitored closely by management on an individual basis. It is, therefore, probable that they form individual IGUs, even if there are central sales and marketing and finance functions. It is conceivable that a hotel chain that markets itself centrally to perhaps mainly commercial customers, might, as part of its business strategy, operate a loss making hotel in a particularly popular higher cost location in order, for example, to secure group wide contracts or a nationally advertised price pledge. On the other hand, a hotel may operate as part of a small cluster of similar quality hotels that are managed as a single operation and frequently refer guests to each other when one is full. In such circumstances, it might be argued that the hotel's income is not independent and, hence, an IGU is a larger grouping.

Petrol stations

6.20 The income of individual petrol stations is likely to be closely monitored by management, for example to determine the relative impact of local pricing differentials, and costs are likely to be able to be determined to arrive at a measure of profitability. If management would consider closing one station depending upon its individual performance, each petrol station may be an IGU – similar to the restaurant example in the FRS. However, it is unlikely that any one station owned by a major operator would be material. Therefore, where a large number of outlets is involved, impairment reviews would normally be carried out on the basis of groupings affected by the same economic conditions. Where establishments combine retail, catering, hotel and petrol outlets the interdependency of these income streams would also need to be taken into account.

Vertically integrated operations

6.21 The fourth example in the FRS illustrates vertical integration. When determining whether a group of assets involved in an intermediate stage in the production process should be treated as an IGU, the most important factor is to consider the extent to which there is an external market and source of supply for its products. This will help to determine whether the income of one facility is dependent on the income of another.

6.22 If there is a deep and liquid external market and source of supply for each stage of production, the income of each process is likely to be independent in the sense that management will monitor and make decisions about retaining or discontinuing it based on its own performance – for example, a line of production might be closed if its output could be sourced more cheaply externally. Similarly, the income generated at the retail end of the business may not be dependent on the fact that its input is supplied internally, if there are alternative sources. In such circumstances, there could be several IGU's within the vertically integrated operation.

6.23 On the other hand, if there is no external market for the output of a facility in the production chain, or the external market is not of sufficient depth to influence management decisions about the production facility itself, its income cannot be independent because the demand for its products depends entirely or substantially on the demand for the products of the facilities further up the line. In extreme cases, the whole enterprise could be a single IGU, because the income generated by each of its activities is entirely dependent on the demand for the end product.

Allocating assets and liabilities to IGUs

6.24 The carrying amount of each IGU being reviewed for impairment needs to be established. This is done by allocating assets and liabilities to individual IGUs. The carrying amount of an IGU consists of:

- Assets and liabilities that are directly and exclusively attributable to the IGU.

- An allocation of assets and liabilities that are indirectly attributable to more than one IGU (that is, central assets).

- Capitalised goodwill (or negative goodwill).

6.25 The assets and liabilities attributed to IGUs should be consistent with the cash flows that are identified for calculating value in use. Assets in the first category above will include all directly attributable tangible and intangible fixed assets and current assets such as stocks, trade debtors and prepayments. Liabilities will include trade creditors and directly attributable accruals and provisions. However, if it is easier in practice to exclude items of working capital in the IGU's balance sheet at the date of the impairment review (that is, items such as trade debtors and creditors that will generate cash flows equal to their carrying amounts), this is permitted provided, of course, that the receipts and payments are also excluded from the value in use calculation.

6.26 Liabilities that relate to financing the operations of IGUs (including interest-bearing debt, dividends and interest payable) are not allocated, because the related cash outflows are also excluded from the impairment calculations and such items are taken into account in the rate used to discount the future operating cash flows when calculating an IGU's value in use. Similarly, tax balances are not allocated, because the discounted cash flow forecasts are prepared on a pre-tax basis.

6.27 The standard does not specify how leased assets should be treated. Under the standard's impairment review methodology, the approach would be as follows. For finance leases, the carrying value of the leased asset would be included in the carrying value of the IGU; the lease liability and the lease payments would be excluded from the impairment calculations because they relate to financing. For operating leases, no assets would be recognised in the carrying value of the IGU; the lease payments would be treated as operating cash outflows in the calculation of value in use.

Central assets

6.28 Where practicable, FRS 11 requires that assets that contribute indirectly to IGUs (such as corporate head offices, computer centres or research facilities) should be allocated to individual IGUs on a logical and systematic basis that reflects the extent to which those resources are applied to support each IGU. An example is given of pro-rating according to the carrying values of the net assets directly attributable to IGUs. The idea is that the carrying values of all IGUs in a group should add up to the carrying value of the group's net assets in aggregate (excluding tax and financing items) – thus no assets should escape attention in an impairment review.

6.29 The reason for including central assets (which may not generate any income) is that unless the operating assets or IGUs are expected to generate sufficient cash flows to recover the carrying amounts of all the entity's assets (that is, including the central assets which generate no external income themselves), there is an impairment.

6.30 This treatment of central assets may be problematical if companies' information systems do not readily provide such allocations. In addition, the basis for allocating central costs to operating units will need to be reviewed to ensure that the cash flows used for the impairment reviews are on a basis that is consistent with the basis on which the central assets have been allocated.

6.31 By including allocations of central assets within the IGU's carrying value, the impairment review checks whether or not the IGU's net cash flows (exclusive of any cash outflows relating to the IGU's use of those central assets) are expected to recover the carrying values of the IGU's own assets and the allocated portion of central assets. For example, if an IGU is allocated a portion of the book value of the group's thead office, the impairment review compares the IGU's value in use with the carrying value as increased. Any internal charges that are payable relating to the use of the head office would need to be excluded from the IGU's cash flows; otherwise the consumption of head office resources would be double-counted, because the carrying value would be increased and the value in use decreased by the same item.

6.32 FRS 11 permits a simpler alternative approach to be used where central assets cannot readily be allocated on a meaningful basis. The alternative approach permits central assets to be reviewed for impairment on an aggregate basis where there is no reasonable basis for allocating them to individual IGUs. This would require a two-tier impairment review:

■　A review at the individual IGU level, where only the assets and liabilities directly involved are reviewed for impairment.

■　A review at a higher level, where any central assets that contribute to the relevant IGU are reviewed for impairment in aggregate with all other IGUs to which they contribute. This review compares the aggregate of the net assets of those IGUs and the central assets with their combined value in use.

6.33　A consequence of this approach is that impairment tests encompass certain IGUs irrespective of whether they are displaying characteristics which would trigger an impairment review.

6.34　The two methods described above of dealing with central assets are likely to result in different impairment calculations. The second method of not allocating central assets to IGUs reduces the prospect of impairment losses being identified. The reason is that impairment losses that may otherwise be attributed to individual IGUs (because their carrying values would reflect allocations of central assets) may to some extent be avoided if the carrying amounts of central assets can be recovered from other more profitable IGUs. At the IGU level, there is no impairment of the operating assets as long as they are earning a market-related return on their carrying values. At the combined level, there is no impairment of the central assets as long as the combined operations are in aggregate earning a market-related return on all the assets, including the central assets. An example in chapter 8 illustrates the different calculations.

Purchased goodwill

6.35　For goodwill, the details of the impairment review differ according to whether:

■   Goodwill *only* is being reviewed for impairment (for example, the mandatory annual review for goodwill with a useful life of more than 20 years, where there are no indicators of impairment).

■   Goodwill *and* other fixed assets are being reviewed for impairment (for example, because there are indicators that an impairment may have occurred).

6.36   The differences relate to the level of aggregation at which groups of assets or businesses are reviewed for impairment. Although impairment reviews for fixed assets, including recognised intangibles, should be carried out at the level of each IGU that is being tested for impairment (subject to possible groupings on materiality grounds), FRS 11 allows a higher level of aggregation for impairment reviews on goodwill.

6.37   IGUs may be combined for testing the recoverability of the related goodwill if:

■   they were acquired as part of the same investment; and
■   they are involved in similar parts of the business.
[FRS 11 para 34].

6.38   This means that if goodwill relating to the acquisition of a group of companies has to be reviewed annually for impairment only because it is being carried permanently as an asset or is being amortised over more than 20 years, and there are no reasons to suggest that either the goodwill or other assets have actually been impaired, the whole acquisition could be treated as one IGU for the purpose of testing goodwill for impairment if the acquisition comprises similar activities. Thus, the overall goodwill on the acquisition would not have to be sub-divided for the purpose of this impairment review.

6.39   If, however, there are indicators that the carrying values of goodwill or fixed assets may not be recoverable, the normal rules of FRS 11 apply. Individual reviews of each relevant IGU must then be carried out to consider whether fixed assets (other than goodwill) have been impaired.

6.40 If IGUs are combined for testing goodwill, a two-tier impairment review is required, similar to the combined approach for dealing with central assets:

- A review at the individual IGU level, where the assets and liabilities (excluding any allocation of goodwill) are reviewed for impairment. Any impairment loss is attributed to the IGU's assets.

- A review at a higher level to test the recoverability of the goodwill, where all the IGUs to which the goodwill relates are reviewed in aggregate. This review compares the carrying amount of the net assets of those IGUs and the purchased goodwill in aggregate with their combined value in use. Any further impairment loss identified at this level relates to the goodwill.

An example illustrating the two different approaches to treating goodwill is given in chapter 8.

Guidelines on allocating goodwill

6.41 The carrying amount of capitalised goodwill should be allocated either to individual IGUs or, if the alternative approach is taken, to groups of similar IGUs that formed part of the same acquisition. An impairment of goodwill in one business could not be offset against an increase in value of another dissimilar business or one that was acquired at a different time.

6.42 Groups need to keep detailed records of the composition of the aggregate amount of purchased goodwill, that is, to which parts of the group it relates. Apart from the possibility of impairment reviews in the future, allocation of goodwill to business units is necessary to account for subsequent disposals (to determine how much goodwill should be written off when a business is sold) and to keep track of elements of goodwill with different useful economic lives.

6.43   It has always been recognised that there are practical difficulties with attributing goodwill to businesses closed or sold. Tracing purchased goodwill is an issue in complex group structures, particularly where an acquired business quickly loses its separate identity or when businesses undergo change and restructuring. Nevertheless, groups have generally managed to make reasonable allocations of goodwill to disposals.

6.44   As far as is practical and consistent with the requirements of the impairment review, the objective should be to allocate goodwill balances to business units on a basis consistent with the group's management reporting structure.

6.45   There is no real guidance in the accounting standards dealing with goodwill and impairment on how to allocate purchased goodwill to different business units. In principle, goodwill should be allocated based on information and factors existing at the date of acquisition. A reasonable guideline is found in US GAAP, where such allocations to each business unit should be completed within the hindsight period for completing the fair value exercise. In addition, FAS 121, 'Accounting for the impairment of long-lived assets and for long-lived assets to be disposed of', requires that when fixed assets are tested for recoverability, any related goodwill should be allocated to the business units on a pro-rata basis using the relative fair values of the fixed assets and recognised intangibles acquired at the acquisition date, unless there is evidence to suggest that some other method of associating the goodwill with those assets is more appropriate.

6.46   If the acquirer, when framing its offer, had assessed individually the values of different businesses in an acquired group, such valuations should be a good starting point for the allocation of goodwill. Thereafter, various methods could be adopted to apportion goodwill to different IGUs or groups of similar IGUs. The choice should best reflect the basis on which the business would be valued by the market at the time of the acquisition. It should be noted, however, that FRS 10 does not permit purchased goodwill arising on a single acquisition transaction to be divided into components of positive and negative goodwill, because goodwill (positive or negative) is treated as a residual difference that arises from fair valuing the acquisition as a whole. Examples of possible allocation methods are:

■ Using discounted cash flow forecasts where these are available at the time of the acquisition.

■ Pro-rata on the basis of a price-earnings formula, using cash flows or income streams projected at the acquisition date.

■ Pro-rata on net asset value at the acquisition date (probably excluding interest-bearing debt and other financing liabilities).

■ Pro-rata using the fair values of the fixed assets at the acquisition date.

6.47 Earnings-based methods may give a very different goodwill allocation from asset-based methods. The choice would be determined by ascertaining how the market rates businesses similar to those acquired – on an earnings or net assets basis. Earnings-based methods are, in general, likely to be appropriate for most acquisitions, because asset-based methods do not generally reflect the relative profitability of different businesses. A cash flow/PE approach is also consistent with the principles for calculating value in use. An asset value basis would be appropriate for some asset-based acquisitions, such as property companies.

6.48 The choice of a price-earnings ratio could be influenced by considering PE ratios of similar businesses that are quoted. For example, if an acquisition comprised a construction and a transport operation, the allocation would take account of the differing PE ratios relating to those sectors at the acquisition date.

6.49 Where an acquisition gives rise to positive goodwill overall, no goodwill (positive or negative) would be attributed to an IGU where management believe none existed when the group was acquired. For example, where a business is loss-making or operating at a low level of profitability that does not cover the cost of capital, no negative goodwill should be allocated; instead, the overall goodwill on the acquisition would be allocated to those IGUs where it is believed goodwill does exist.

6.50 An example of different allocation methods is illustrated below.

Example – allocation of purchased goodwill

An acquisition of a group comprises three business segments A, B and C. Total purchase consideration was £450m. The fair value of the net assets in aggregate was £350m (as allocated in the table below), leaving goodwill of £100m. Different allocation methods are illustrated in the table below.

Business acquired	A	B	C	Total
Profit estimate	20	30	(5)	45
Net assets – fair value	200	100	50	350
Sector PE ratio	12	8		
Goodwill – earnings basis	22	78	Nil	100
Goodwill – net assets basis	67	33	Nil	100

Segment C (which is loss-making) receives a zero allocation of goodwill under both methods. Therefore, all of the goodwill has been allocated to A and B.

On an earnings basis, A and B are each valued at £240m (that is, 12 × £20m and 8 × £30m respectively), compared with fair valued net assets of £200m and £100m respectively. The purchased goodwill of £100m is allocated *pro rata* to the amount by which the values of A and B exceed the fair values of their net assets (£40m and £140m respectively) which results in £22m being allocated to A and £78m being allocated to B.

On a net assets basis, the purchased goodwill of £100m is allocated pro rata to the fair valued net assets of £200m in A and £100m in B, which results in £67m being allocated to A and £33m to B.

6.51 In the above example, no goodwill (positive or negative) has been allocated to segment C, which is loss-making. FRS 10 does not allow both positive and negative goodwill to be recognised in respect of a single acquisition. If the assets of that business are already impaired at the date of acquisition, FRS 7 requires the impairment to be reflected by reducing the fair values on acquisition. [FRS 7 paras 47, 49].

Income-generating units

Chapter 7

Calculating value in use

Composition of cash flow forecasts

7.1   Estimating value in use involves identifying the future cash flows that are expected to arise from the fixed asset or IGU (or group of IGUs) being tested for impairment. The cash flows consist of those expected to arise from the continued use of the asset or IGU and those, if any, expected to result from its ultimate disposal.

7.2   Relevant cash flow forecasts should be made on the basis of reasonable and supportable assumptions and should be consistent with the most up-to-date budgets and plans that have been formally approved by management. [FRS 11 para 36]. However, the detailed requirements include a number of exceptions to that principle, which have the effect of constraining the rate of growth and anticipated improvements that may be built into the assumptions. These are considered from paragraph 7.14 below.

7.3   The period covered by cash flow forecasts must obviously relate to the useful lives of the fixed assets or goodwill being reviewed for impairment. However, periods covered by detailed formal budgets and plans will vary in different companies and industries. In some, cash flows cannot be predicted with much certainty beyond short periods. The useful lives of the assets concerned may extend far beyond the period covered by formal budgets and plans. It is then necessary to extrapolate the formal cash flow projections into the future using reasonable and prudent broad assumptions about growth and future prospects. The standard places constraints on those assumptions that should be complied with in most circumstances and controls those assumptions by requirements for disclosure where higher growth rates are assumed.

7.4   Where the carrying value of an IGU includes goodwill or other fixed assets with an indefinite useful economic life, the calculation of value in use will include an estimated value of the IGU's cash flows relating to the indefinite period beyond that covered by detailed cash flow projections. This may be calculated by applying a terminal value multiple to, say, the cash flows expected in the last year covered by the company's explicit forecasts, by using the formula *1/r-g*, where *r* is the discount rate and *g* is the estimated longer term annual rate of growth in the cash flows (constraints on long-term growth rates are considered from para 7.16). The terminal value calculated as at the end of the period covered by formal budgets and plans will, of course, have to be discounted to its present value.

7.5   The composition of the cash flows that are used to estimate value in use needs to be considered carefully. It is important, for example, to ensure that they are comparable with the basis on which the carrying amounts of the IGUs have been established, so that omissions or double-countings that would lead to errors in the calculations are avoided.

7.6   The cash flows will include:

■   Cash inflows from the use of the asset or the activities of the IGU.

■   Cash outflows directly attributable to the asset or IGU.

■   Any allocation of cash flows attributable to central overheads.

■   Net cash inflows expected from the disposal of assets or IGUs at the end of their useful lives.

■   Cash outflows to maintain the operating capacity of existing fixed assets.

7.7   The cash flows should exclude cash flows relating to financing (which include interest payments), since financing items are also excluded from the liabilities attributed to IGUs and because the cost of capital is taken into account by discounting the cash flows. Tax cash flows should also be excluded, because the FRS requires value in use to be calculated on the basis of discounting pre-tax cash flows at a pre-tax discount rate (in practice, however, value in use if often likely to be derived from post-tax cash flows discounted at a post-tax discount rate, as discussed from para 7.46).

7.8   Cash inflows and outflows relating to working capital (that is, items such as trade debtors and creditors that are expected to generate cash flows equal to their carrying amounts) in the balance sheet at the time of the impairment review can be excluded from the calculations if that is easier than allocating the working capital components to individual IGUs. The assets and liabilities are then excluded from the carrying value of the IGU and the respective receipts and payments are also excluded from the value in use calculation. [FRS 11 para 33]. In practice, companies may find it easier to prepare an operating profit forecast for the IGU being tested for impairment and then to convert the operating profit forecast into a cash flow forecast by carrying out the same sort of reconciliation of operating profit to operating cash flow as specified in FRS 1, 'Cash flow statements'.

Transfer pricing between IGUs

7.9   Internal transfer pricing directly affects the cash inflows and operating cash outflows relating to separate IGUs in, say, vertically integrated groups. For example, consider a situation where one IGU transfers part of its output to another IGU in the same group at a price that is lower than the market price for its output. This issue is not addressed directly in FRS 11, however, the fourth mini-case study in the standard that discusses how IGUs are determined in vertically integrated groups (see chapter 6) indicates that the cash inflows of the transferor IGU and the cash outflows of the transferee IGU that are used in the value in use calculations should be adjusted to reflect market prices rather than internal transfer prices.

7.10 This principle of adjusting cash flows to reflect market prices, which is stated more explicitly in IAS 36, is logical if the cash inflows of both business units are properly to be regarded as independent. Otherwise, either the wrong assets (in terms of their true economic value to the business) could be identified as being impaired, or impairments might be avoided altogether purely by making adjustments to internal transfer prices. This is likely to be a subjective area in practice.

Central overheads

7.11 The inclusion in the cash flow forecasts of central overheads is mentioned only briefly in FRS 11, which notes that the cash flows include *"any allocation of central overheads"*. [FRS 11 para 36]. It is reasonable to assume that the cash outflows attributable to an IGU should include sensible allocations of central overheads, in the same way that the carrying values of IGUs should, where practicable, include apportionments of central assets. The assets of an IGU could be considered to be impaired if, for example, its own cash flows did not make a contribution to central overheads that are incurred to support its activities.

7.12 It is important to ensure that central overheads are not omitted altogether in the value in use calculations. It is also important to ensure that central assets and overheads are not double-counted in the impairment review. For example, if part of the carrying value of head office property is allocated to IGUs for the purpose of impairment reviews, any internal management charges that are rendered to IGUs relating to the use of that property should be excluded from their cash outflows – otherwise, the carrying value of the IGU would be increased and its value in use decreased by elements relating to the same item.

Inflation

7.13 Assumptions about inflation can be dealt with in one of two ways. One method is to forecast cash flows in current prices – that is, not to forecast future inflation. The cash flows are then discounted at a real discount rate (that is, a rate of return that excludes inflation). The second method is to forecast cash flows to include estimates of inflation in revenues and costs. The cash flows are then discounted at a nominal discount rate (that is, a rate of return that includes inflation). It is important that inflation is treated consistently in the cash flow projections and the choice of discount rate. [FRS 11 para 46].

Constraints on forecasts

7.14 FRS 11 imposes several important limitations on the cash flows that may be recognised in the calculation of value in use, including restrictions on the growth assumptions that can be built into long-term cash flow forecasts.

Growth rates

7.15 In the period that is covered by formal budgets and plans, there are no restrictions as long as the period does not exceed five years. Therefore, in that initial period the cash flows will reflect the variability in growth rates that is included in the explicit forecasts.

7.16 However, the cash flows for periods beyond those covered by formal budgets and plans (whether they cover the full five years or a shorter period) should assume a steady or declining growth rate that does not exceed the long-term average growth rate for the country or countries in which the business operates. The UK's post-war average growth in gross domestic product, expressed in real terms (that is, assuming no inflation), is stated to be 2.25 per cent. Furthermore, the period before the steady or declining growth rate is assumed should not normally exceed five years. Only in exceptional circumstances may this growth constraint be overridden, with appropriate disclosure. [FRS 11 para 36].

7.17 Whilst this restriction is clearly aimed at preventing short-term difficulties from being overridden by over-optimistic long-term forecasts, the theory is that in the long run a business has no right to assume it can out-perform the economy as a whole. It is also prudent in the light of an uncertain future.

7.18 The FRS gives an example of a situation where a higher long-term growth rate may be justified. This is where the specific industry is expected to grow faster than the country's economy in the long-term and the business under review is expected to grow as rapidly as the industry as a whole, taking into account the prospects of increased competition. [FRS 11 para 37]. However, the ASB issues a caution in the development section of the FRS that, in its view, individual businesses in higher growth industries do not necessarily grow as quickly as the industry, because such industries may attract new businesses, reducing the opportunities for high growth rates in existing businesses.

7.19 Where the long-term growth rate assumed in the calculation of value in use for the period beyond that covered by explicit forecasts exceeds the long-term average for the country in which the business operates, the assumed growth rate and the circumstances justifying it must be disclosed. [FRS 11 para 73].

7.20 There may be situations where it would be unrealistic to cap the growth assumptions (that is, defaulting to a restricted steady or declining growth rate) after five years. This might be the case where hi-tech businesses are purchased at high multiples of current earnings, reflecting longer term growth prospects. For example, a recently acquired IGU with products under development may be expected to incur losses for two or three years and be followed by several years of significant growth as the new products reach the market – thus cash flow forecasts with explicit growth assumptions may exceed five years. But the circumstances for overriding the presumed five year cut-off must be exceptional and must be disclosed.

7.21 Where, in the calculation of value in use, the period covered by explicit forecasts and before a steady or declining growth rate is assumed exceeds five years, FRS 11 requires the length of the longer period and the circumstances justifying it to be disclosed. [FRS 11 para 72].

'Look-back' tests

7.22 FRS 11 contains a safety net to safeguard against entities continually using over-optimistic forecasts to defer impairment losses. Where an impairment review has been carried out and recoverable amount has been based on value in use, the standard requires the results of the review to be monitored for the next five years, irrespective of whether or not an impairment loss was booked when the review was carried out. [FRS 11 para 54].

7.23 The actual cash flows should be compared with those forecast in the impairment review. If actual cash flows are significantly less than those previously forecast, the calculations should be re-performed by substituting the actual cash flows for those previously forecast. In this exercise, forecasts of future cash flows should remain as previously forecast in the original impairment review, except for where actual cash flows are lower than previously forecast, because certain cash inflows or outflows have occurred, or will occur, in an earlier or later period than was budgeted. If the reworked calculation identifies a previously unrecognised impairment (or increases a previously recognised impairment), an immediate impairment write-down should be made in the current period.

7.24 The under-performance in the years following the original impairment review might be an indicator of further impairment losses and, hence, a new impairment review will also be required, reflecting *current* budgets and plans. Any further impairment losses identified should be recognised immediately.

7.25 There is, however, an exception to the requirement for an immediate write-down when the exercise described above identifies an impairment. A new impairment review, reflecting *current* budgets and plans, might indicate that the impairment loss identified when the original impairment calculations were re-performed no longer exists. In this situation, an impairment loss is deemed to have arisen (based on the original calculations as reworked) and reversed (based on the new forecasts of value in use). If the reasons for the turnaround meet FRS 11's criteria for reversing previously recognised impairment losses, a write-down is not required. Instead, the impairment that would have been recognised and its subsequent reversal should be disclosed. [FRS 11 para 71].

7.26 The following example illustrates the calculations.

Example

At 31 December 20X1, an asset with a carrying value of £500,000 and a remaining useful economic life of 5 years was reviewed for impairment. Its recoverable amount was based on value in use of £506,000 and so no impairment loss was recognised.

In years 20X2 and 20X3 the actual net cash flows were significantly lower than forecast. In accordance with FRS 11 (para 54), the original value in use calculations are reworked using the actual net cash flows, as illustrated in the table below. The original value in use is recalculated as £450,000.

The future cash flows have been discounted at a rate of 5%. For simplicity, it has been assumed that the cash flows arise at the end of each year.

Year	Review at 20X1		Review re-performed at 20X3	
	Future net cash flows £000	Present value £000	Future net cash flows £000	Present value £000
20X2	100	95	90*	85
20X3	110	100	60*	54
20X4	120	103	120	103
20X5	130	106	130	106
20X6	130	102	130	102
Value in use		506		450

* Actual cash flows

The revised calculation of value in use (£450,000) as at 31 December 20X1 indicates an impairment loss of £50,000 compared to the carrying value of £500,000. The impairment loss should be recognised in the year ended 31 December 20X3.

Part of the impairment loss of £50,000 would have been charged as depreciation in years 20X2 and 20X3. FRS 11 does not specify how such depreciation should be taken into account. A suggested method is shown in the table below, which indicates that an impairment loss of £30,000 is required at 31 December 20X3 after adjusting for depreciation, in order to write the asset down from its carrying value of £300,000 to the carrying value that would have been recognised if the impairment loss of £50,000 had been booked at 31 December 20X1.

	Carrying value before impairment	Carrying value after impairment
	£000	£000
31 December X1	500	500
Impairment loss	-	(50)
Depreciation 20X2 and 20X3	(200)	(180)
31 December X3	300	270

It should be noted that a further impairment review may be necessary at 31 December 20X3. Value in use would be calculated using management's latest forecasts of future cash flows. Any further impairment loss thus identified should be recognised immediately.

If the current estimate of value in use exceeds the impaired carrying value of £270,000, the impairment loss should not be reversed, unless the increase in value in use results from a forecast change in economic conditions or in the expected use of the asset. [FRS 11 para 56]. Thus in this example, if management's latest cash flow forecasts for the 3 years to 31 December 20X6 were in line with the previous estimates (£120,000, £130,000 and £130,000 respectively), their present value (that is, value in use) at 31 December 20X3 would be £345,000. Although value in use of £345,000 exceeds the impaired carrying value of £270,000, no reversal of the impairment loss is permitted, because the increase in value in use arises solely from the reduced net cash flows in years 20X2 and 20X3 now having past and from the discounted value of the future cash flows having increased (see further chapter 9).

Reorganisation and capital expenditure

7.27 A key – and controversial – constraint concerning the assumptions in the cash flow forecasts relates to future reorganisation and capital investment. Value in use is supposed to reflect the value of assets or goodwill in their current condition. Hence, the future costs and benefits of future reorganisations should not be recognised in the cash flow forecasts, unless related provisions have been made. Furthermore, the costs and benefits of future capital investment that is intended to improve or enhance the performance of the assets or business should not be taken into account in the cash flow forecasts. [FRS 11 para 38].

7.28 These are severe constraints on the calculations. Impairment reviews should be based on the most recent budgets and plans that have been formally approved by management. Where management has approved reorganisation and capital investment plans, however, the most recent formally approved budgets and plans would typically include both the costs and benefits (such as lower production costs or extra revenues from higher quality output) of the planned reorganisation and capital expenditure. Provisions for reorganisation costs might, however, be recognised in financial statements later than their inclusion in formal budgets and plans – say, after the balance sheet date at which assets are being reviewed for impairment.

7.29 FRS 12, 'Provisions, contingent liabilities and contingent assets', sets out in some detail the conditions that must be complied with before provisions for reorganisations may be recognised in financial statements. In particular, FRS 12 states that a management or board decision to restructure that is taken before the balance sheet date does not give rise to a constructive obligation (the trigger for recognising a provision) unless the entity has, before the balance sheet date (a) started to implement the restructuring, or (b) announced its main features to those affected by it in a sufficiently specific manner to raise a valid expectation in them that the entity will carry out the restructuring.

7.30 If those criteria are met by the balance sheet date and the costs have been provided for in the financial statements, the expenditure and the related benefits (such as savings from lower staff costs) of the reorganisation should also be included in the cash flow forecasts in the appropriate period for determining value in use.

7.31 If, however, those criteria are not met by the balance sheet date and, therefore, no provisions for reorganisation costs have been booked, the costs and benefits of the reorganisation should not be taken into account in the calculation of value in use either. To comply with FRS 11, it is necessary to strip out of the formally approved budgets and plans the planned expenditure on restructuring and the related benefits.

7.32 Stripping out the cash inflows and outflows relating to a planned reorganisation or improvement-type capital expenditure may not be straightforward. For example, it is hypothetical to forecast what future revenues would be if the business remained static rather than being developed in the way that is envisaged and so it may be difficult to adjust a budget to show what the cash flows would be estimated to be if a planned reorganisation or capital expenditure did not take place.

Future reorganisation

7.33 The following example illustrates the treatment of a future reorganisation and the interaction of the impairment calculations with the recognition of reorganisation provisions. The example contrasts the timing of impairment losses and reorganisation costs, which differ according to whether or not the reorganisation is sufficiently advanced in its execution for provisions to be recognised in the financial statements. It also shows how the rules may give rise to the recognition of impairment losses in earlier periods, even though management may expect to avoid impairment by reorganisation, and the reversal of such impairment losses in later periods when the reorganisation is implemented.

Example – future reorganisation planned

At 31 December 20X1, the assets and goodwill of an income-generating unit are being reviewed for impairment. The carrying value of the IGU's net assets is £6,500,000 (excluding any reorganisation provision) and the remaining useful economic life of the recognised assets is 8 years.

Management's approved budgets at 31 December 20X1 include reorganisation costs of £350,000 to be incurred in 20X2; the reorganisation is expected to generate cost savings of £100,000 per annum from 20X3 onwards. Formal budgets have been prepared for the three years to 31 December 20X4; thereafter, for the purpose of the impairment review, a zero growth rate is assumed, because market conditions are extremely competitive and this is expected to continue for the foreseeable future. The future cash flow estimates are set out below, along with figures that exclude from those estimates the cost and benefits of the planned reorganisation. Thus in 20X2 the net cash flows without reorganisation (£870,000) exceed the net cash flows with reorganisation (£520,000) by the amount of the reorganisation costs (£350,000).

The future cash flows (which exclude inflation) have been discounted at a rate of 4%. For simplicity, it has been assumed that the cash flows arise at the end of each year; therefore, the figures in the 'present value' columns for the cash flows (CF) in 'n' years time from 31 December 20X1 are derived from the formula $CF^n/(1+i)^n$, where i (the discount rate) is 0.04.

Year	With reorganisation		Without reorganisation	
	Future net cash flows £000	Present value £000	Future net cash flows £000	Present value £000
20X2	520	500	870	836
20X3	1,000	925	900	832
20X4	1,050	933	950	845
20X5	1,050	898	950	812
20X6	1,050	863	950	781
20X7	1,050	830	950	751
20X8	1,050	798	950	722
20X9	1,050	767	950	694
Value in use		6,514		6,273

The impairment calculations at 31 December 20X1 differ according to whether or not provision for the reorganisation costs is recognised in the financial statements.

A – Provision for reorganisation costs recognised at 31 December 20X1

If provision has been made for reorganisation costs, the costs and benefits of the reorganisation are taken into account in determining the IGU's value in use. In this example, the post-reorganisation value in use (£6,514,000) exceeds the IGU's carrying value (£6,500,000 less reorganisation provision £350,000). Hence, there is no impairment of the IGU's assets.

In the year to 31 December 20X1, the financial statements reflect the following charges:

Reorganisation provision	£350,000
Impairment loss	Nil

B – No provision for reorganisation costs recognised at 31 December 20X1

If no provision for reorganisation costs is permitted by FRS 12, the costs and benefits of the reorganisation have to be stripped out of the projections in determining the IGU's value in use. In this example, the IGU's carrying value (£6,500,000) exceeds its pre-reorganisation value in use (£6,273,000). Therefore, there is an impairment loss of £227,000.

In the year to 31 December 20X1, the financial statements reflect the following charges:

Impairment loss	£227,000
Reorganisation provision	Nil

In the year to 31 December 20X2, the reorganisation is carried out. Assuming that the cash flow projections at 31 December 20X2 are the same as those previously estimated at 31 December 20X1 (including the benefits of the reorganisation), the calculation of the IGU's value in use at 31 December 20X2 is as follows. Note that the present values of each year's cash flows have increased from the previous table because they are one year closer.

Year	Future net cash flows £000	Present value £000
20X3	1,000	961
20X4	1,050	971
20X5	1,050	933
20X6	1,050	897
20X7	1,050	863
20X8	1,050	830
20X9	1,050	798
Value in use		6,253

As a result of the reorganisation, the IGU's value in use at 31 December 20X2 (£6,253,000) will exceed its impaired carrying value (£6,273,000 less depreciation charged in the year). For example, assume the carrying value of the IGU comprises fixed assets as follows, which are depreciated uniformly over their remaining useful life of eight years.

	Depreciated historical cost before impairment £000	Carrying value after impairment £000
31 December X1	6,500	6,273
Depreciation	812	784
31 December X2	5,688	5,489
Value in use		6,253

The IGU's value in use at 31 December 20X2 exceeds the impaired carrying value by £764,000, therefore the impairment loss of £227,000 should be reversed insofar as permitted by FRS 11. Impairment losses should be reversed in situations where the recoverable amount increases as a result of a reorganisation, the benefits of which had been excluded from the original measurement of value in use. [FRS 11 paras 56,57]. In this case, the impairment loss should be reversed by increasing the carrying value of the fixed assets to what it would have been had no impairment loss been recognised in the previous year, that is, from £5,489,000 to £5,688,000 – a reversal of £199,000.

In the year to 31 December 20X2, the financial statements reflect the following charges and credits:

Reorganisation costs	£350,000
Reversal of impairment loss	£199,000 CR

Future capital expenditure

7.34 Future capital expenditure and the related benefits should also be excluded from the calculation of value in use to the extent that the expenditure *"will improve or enhance the income-generating units or assets in excess of their originally assessed standard of performance"*. [FRS 11 para 38]. It should be noted that only improvement-type capital expenditure should be excluded; that which is necessary to maintain an asset or IGU at its originally assessed standard of performance should be included.

7.35 This treatment of capital expenditure needs to be considered carefully. For an individual fixed asset that is being reviewed for impairment, the treatment is relatively straightforward. The value in use takes into account the expenditure that is necessary to maintain the asset for its estimated useful economic life, but it does not anticipate the asset's enhancement or replacement. When those events occur, they result in new capital expenditure being recognised – until then, only the old asset exists.

7.36 FRS 15 codifies the accounting treatment of subsequent expenditure on fixed assets. FRS 15 sets out the circumstances where such expenditure should be capitalised or expensed in the profit and loss account. Repairs and maintenance-type expenditure (that is, expenditure necessary to ensure that an asset maintains its previously assessed standard of performance during its estimated useful life) should be recognised in the profit and loss account as incurred. Such expenditure should be included in the value in use calculations.

7.37 Capitalisation is required in three specific situations. The first is expenditure that enhances the fixed asset in excess of the previously assessed standard of performance. Under FRS 11, the costs and benefits of enhancing assets in excess of the previously assessed standard of performance should be excluded from the impairment calculations.

7.38 The second situation is expenditure that replaces or restores a separate component of the fixed asset (that is, depreciated separately from the rest of the asset). It is highly unlikely that the component would be tested individually for impairment, since it forms part of a larger asset or IGU.

Example

The carrying value of a furnace is being reviewed for impairment. The furnace has a useful life of 20 years and requires relining every 5 years. The lining is treated as a separate asset component under FRS 15. Thus the cost of the lining is depreciated over 5 years; the remainder of the furnace is depreciated over 20 years.

For calculating the furnace's value in use, the net cash flows forecast for the remainder of the furnace's 20 year useful life would include the costs relating to relining the furnace every 5 years, because that expenditure is necessary to maintain the originally assessed standard of performance of the furnace.

7.39 The third situation is expenditure that relates to a major inspection or overhaul of a fixed asset that restores the economic benefits of the asset that have consumed and already reflected in depreciation charges.

Example

An aircraft with a useful life of 20 years requires a major overhaul every 3 years. The value in use of the aircraft would include the costs of each major overhaul (and revenues that assume that the overhauls are carried out and that the aircraft can continue to carry passengers for the whole of its useful economic life).

7.40   The following example illustrates the value in use calculations for an asset where future improvement-type capital expenditure is planned.

Example – improvement-type capital expenditure

A cruise ship is being reviewed for impairment at 31 December 20X1. The ship forms an IGU of its own. Its carrying value is £72,000,000 and its estimated remaining useful life is 10 years, with a residual value estimated at £6,000,000. Management has approved a major investment plan to increase the ship's passenger capacity and to replace its engines. The work will be carried out in 20X4 and is expected to result in a significant increase in passenger revenues and a decrease in running costs. The remaining useful life is expected to be extended by two years. The estimated cost of the new investment is £8,000,000.

It is assumed that recoverable amount is to be determined by reference to value in use alone. The future cash flow estimates are set out below, along with figures that exclude from those estimates the cost and benefits of the planned capital expenditure. The future cash flows (which exclude inflation) have been discounted at a rate of 6%. For simplicity, it has been assumed that the cash flows arise at the end of each year; therefore, the figures in the 'present value' columns for the cash flows (CF) in 'n' years time from 31 December 20X1 are derived from the formula $CF^n/(1+i)^n$, where i (the discount rate) is 0.06.

Year	Including new capex		Excluding new capex	
	Future net cash flows £000	Present value £000	Future net cash flows £000	Present value £000
20X2	8,300	7,830	8,300	7,830
20X3	8,500	7,565	8,500	7,565
20X4	(4,000)	(3,358)	8,500	7,137
20X5	10,500	8,317	8,500	6,732
20X6	10,800	8,070	8,285	6,191
20X7	11,050	7,790	8,078	5,695
20X8	11,250	7,482	7,876	5,238
20X9	11,450	7,184	7,679	4,818
20Y0	10,990	6,505	7,487	4,431
20Y1	10,550	5,891	13,300	7,427
20Y2	10,130	5,336		
20Y3	15,725	7,815		
Value in use		76,427		63,064

For the purpose of the impairment review at 31 December 20X1, the future capital expenditure and the related benefits should be excluded from the calculation of value in use. On this basis, the estimated value in use of the ship in its existing state (£63,064,000) is lower than its carrying value (£72,000,000) and so an impairment loss of £8,936,000 should be recognised.

In the year to 31 December 20X4, the improvement work is carried out. Assuming that the cash flow projections at 31 December 20X4 are the same as those previously estimated at 31 December 20X1, the calculation of the ship's value in use at 31 December 20X4 is as follows.

Calculating value in use

Year	Future net cash flows £000	Present value £000
20X5	10,500	9,906
20X6	10,800	9,612
20X7	11,050	9,278
20X8	11,250	8,911
20X9	11,450	8,556
20Y0	10,990	7,748
20Y1	10,550	7,016
20Y2	10,130	6,356
20Y3	15,725	9,307
Value in use		76,690

The ship's carrying value at 31 December 20X4 is as follows (straight-line depreciation at 10% per annum to the estimated residual value of £6,000,000 has been assumed).

	Carrying value £000
31 December 20X1	63,064
Depreciation 20X2 to 20X4	(17,119)
Capital expenditure	8,000
31 December 20X4	53,945

The ship's value in use following the improvement exceeds its impaired carrying value. In accordance with paragraph 57 of FRS 11, an increase in the recoverable amount as a result of further capital investment (the benefits of which had been excluded from the original measurement of value in use) should result in a reversal of the original impairment loss at

31 December 20X4. The amount of the reversal is restricted to the extent that the carrying value of the ship is increased to what it would have been had the original impairment not occurred, which is calculated as follows, resulting in a reversal of £6,255,000 (£60,200,000-£53,945,000).

	Carrying value without impairment £000
31 December X1	72,000
Depreciation 20X2 to 20X4	(19,800)
Capital expenditure	8,000
31 December X4	60,200

7.41 Where all the fixed assets and goodwill of an IGU are being reviewed for impairment, the calculation of the IGU's value in use may need to include a level of fixed asset replacement expenditure in the period that is covered by the impairment review. For example, where the assets of an IGU include purchased goodwill with a long estimated useful economic life (in excess of the lives of many of the IGU's fixed assets), the cash flows of the IGU should include a normal level of fixed asset replacement expenditure that is necessary to maintain the operations of the IGU (and, hence, to support its originally assessed revenue-generating capability). However, the value in use of an IGU's existing assets and goodwill does not anticipate the costs of future improvement-type capital expenditure and the related benefits (such as additional revenues or cost savings from the use of more efficient technology). Those items would be factored into an impairment review when the capital expenditure has been incurred and new assets have been recognised, which need to be reviewed for impairment. In practice, the dividing line between maintenance-type and improvement-type capital expenditure is rarely clear-cut, since businesses are not static; the former often includes an element of the latter, especially as regards overhauls and regular refurbishments.

Newly acquired IGUs

7.42 The above rules relating to future reorganisation and capital expenditure are modified for newly acquired IGUs. FRS 11 allows the costs and benefits of planned reorganisation and capital investment relating to a newly acquired IGU to be taken into account for the purpose of impairment reviews in the initial years after the acquisition. In the case of a planned reorganisation, this is irrespective of whether provisions have yet been made in the post-acquisition financial statements (provision for such costs in determining the fair value of the net assets acquired is not permitted by FRS 7). However, the reorganisation or investment that is taken into account in those impairment reviews should be consistent with the budgets and plans that had been formulated by the end of the first full year after the acquisition. [FRS 11 para 39].

7.43 This is a somewhat pragmatic approach for the purpose of reviewing the value of goodwill on a recent acquisition. FRS 10 requires goodwill with a long (more than 20 years) or indefinite life to be reviewed for impairment at the end of each financial year, including the year immediately following the acquisition. Goodwill with a shorter life (20 years or less) should be reviewed for impairment at the end of the first full year following the acquisition. FRS 11's pragmatic approach recognises that purchasers generally share something of the perceived benefits from an acquisition with the vendors. It avoids the situation where goodwill on a new acquisition might be deemed to be impaired (and, hence, written down immediately) solely because the benefits of future reorganisation and investment, which were taken into account by the acquirer in framing its offer, could not be reflected in the impairment reviews over the initial years.

7.44 The FRS goes on to explain that the validity of this treatment would be called into question if the reorganisation or investment does not, in fact, proceed according to the acquisition plan. That situation would itself be an indicator that the assets and goodwill of the acquired business may be impaired and subsequent impairment reviews should then be carried out by excluding the costs and benefits of the originally planned reorganisation or capital investment from the value in use calculations. [FRS 11 para 40].

7.45 The formation of new IGUs in business startup situations is not addressed in the FRS, but the principles described above from the perspective of acquisitions seem appropriatewhere, in order to obtain the benefits from initial investment, it is necessary to undertake further capital expenditure. For example, in the early stages of the development of a new project, an impairment loss might be identified if no account were taken of future capital expenditure required to complete the development plan, as it might be loss-making on a 'current condition' basis (that is, until successful completion). Applying the principles of paragraph 39 of FRS 11, if the projections in the development plan (taking account of future capital expenditure required to enable the IGU to reach its originally assessed standard of performance) showed an adequate expected rate of return on the new investment, there would be no impairment. However, if the business subsequently abandoned the development plan, it could no longer be used to support the avoidance of an impairment loss.

Discount rate

7.46 Investment decisions take account of the time value of money and the risks associated with expected future cash flows. These are also reflected in the measurement of an asset's value in use, which in a sense represents an estimate of what the market would pay for the asset assuming it generated cash flows equivalent to those expected by the entity that controls it.

7.47 The principle is that the expected future cash flows are discounted at a rate described as *"an estimate of the rate that the market would expect on an equally risky investment"*. [FRS 11 para 41]. This rate reflects both current assessments of the time value of money and the risks specific to the asset concerned. This means that (unless net realisable value is higher) an asset is regarded as impaired if it is not expected to earn a current market-related rate of return on its carrying value.

7.48 The rate of return expected by the market is in theory independent of the way the asset is financed, although the entity's overall cost of capital will sometimes provide a good starting point for estimating a rate.

7.49 The choice of a discount rate is a subjective area. Furthermore, the value in use calculations are sensitive to variations in discount rates. Often there is no directly observable market rate. The FRS suggests the market rate can be estimated by a number of means:

- The rate implicit in market transactions of similar assets.

- The weighted average cost of capital (WACC) for a listed company with a similar risk profile.

- The WACC for the entity, adjusted up or down for the particular risks of the IGU being reviewed for impairment.

[FRS 11 para 42].

7.50 Rates applicable to different business units within a group may vary to reflect any risk factors that are specific to those units. Trading activities and investments in different countries are likely to have different risks, for example, currency and political risks. The rate should be appropriate to the country in which the IGU operates (or in whose currency it derives its major cash flows) rather than the country in which the finance is sourced. Different business sectors also attract different risks – for example, a biotechnology company will carry a greater market risk than a regulated utility. In general, the more uncertain the cash flows are, the more risky the investment is, and the greater the risk adjustment is to increase the discount rate.

7.51 For some companies, the WACC will be an observable rate that they are familiar with. IAS 36 refers to using techniques such as the

Capital Asset Pricing Model, which is commonly used in assessing the cost of equity. The FRS notes, however, that if the discount rates are derived from the entity's WACC, the weighted average of the rates applied to each IGU should equal the WACC of the entity as a whole. [FRS 11 para 43]. The FRS does not, however, indicate how this calculation might be performed; proving that the sum of the IGUs' WACCs equals the entity's WACC may be difficult and may not really be relevant if only one IGU is being reviewed for impairment.

7.52 If an impairment loss is recognised and is measured by reference to value in use of a fixed asset or IGU, the FRS also requires the discount rate to be disclosed in the financial statements. As an alternative to using a risk-adjusted discount rate, it may sometimes be more practicable to adjust the expected cash flows (downwards) for risk and to discount those risk-adjusted cash flows at a risk-free discount rate, such as a government bond rate. [FRS 11 para 45]. Where this is done, the FRS requires some indication of the risk-adjustments made to the cash flows to be disclosed. [FRS 11 para 69]. It is important that risk is not double-counted in the calculations; that is, the discount rate should not include a risk weighting if the underlying cash flows have already been adjusted for risk.

7.53 Inflation should also be treated consistently in the present value calculations. If the future cash flows are estimated at current values, the discount rate is a real rate, that is, inflation should be excluded. If the estimated future cash flows include inflation, the discount rate is a nominal rate, that is including inflation.

Pre-tax rate

7.54 FRS 11 requires the discount rate to be calculated on a pre-tax basis. [FRS 11 para 41].Thus an IGU's pre-tax cash flows should be discounted at the determined pre-tax discount rate.

7.55 The use of pre-tax cash flows and a pre-tax discount rate means that any deferred tax arising is provided in the normal way and is not reflected in the carrying amount of the asset. Thus if there is an impairment loss, this creates a timing difference on which deferred tax should be recognised if required by SSAP 15.

7.56 FRS 11 recognises that in many cases the only observable market rate of return is a *post-tax* rate. This is the case, for example, where the discount rate is derived from an entity's WACC, which many companies would look to when estimating the appropriate discount rate. The FRS requires the post-tax rate to be adjusted to a pre-tax basis.

7.57 How to calculate the appropriate *pre-tax* rate from a *post-tax* starting point is a key practical issue. It is not simply a matter of grossing up the required post-tax rate of return at the standard or effective rate of tax and discounting the pre-tax cash flows at that grossed up rate.

7.58 Appendix 1 to the standard gives some guidance on how the adjustment to a pre-tax rate might be calculated. It states that the required pre-tax rate is *"the rate of return that will, after tax has been deducted, give the required post-tax rate of return"*. The example given in the standard is over-simplified, but some useful observations can be drawn from it.

Example – FRS 11 grossing up

The post-tax market rate of return required from an asset is 14%. Profits are taxed at 30%; there is a capital allowance of 100% of the cost of the asset. All cash flows arise at the end of year 1.

For an asset costing £100, the required post-tax cash flows during year 1 are £114. Pre-tax cash flows of £120 must be earned in order to give the required post-tax return of £114. Pre-tax cash flows of £120 result in a tax charge of £6 – comprising tax on profit before depreciation of £36 (30% of £120) less tax relief on the cost of the asset of £30 (30% of £100). Thus the required pre-tax rate is 20%.

The value in use of £100 of an asset with the above cash flows can be derived either by discounting the post-tax cash flows of £114 at the post-tax rate of 14% or by discounting the pre-tax cash flows of £120 at the derived pre-tax rate of 20%. The same answer is obtained from both methods, because the cost of the asset is fully deductible for tax purposes as a result of the 100% capital allowances and, therefore, does not give rise to any timing differences.

7.59 It can be seen from the above example that the pre-tax rate has to be derived from the post-tax rate and the post-tax cash flows. Therefore, the starting point is a *post-tax* analysis, despite the value in use calculation being labelled as a pre-tax exercise. This is not surprising since investment appraisals are generally done at a post-tax level.

7.60 It should be noted that in this example, grossing up from a post-tax rate of 14 per cent to a pre-tax rate of 20 per cent reflects the assumed rate of corporation tax only because of its unreal simplicity. The relationship between the post-tax rate and the derived pre-tax rate will deviate from the standard rate as soon as real factors are introduced such as uneven multi-period cash flows, timing differences between pre-tax cash flows and the related tax cash flows and so on.

7.61 At inception, in the absence of any impairment, the pre-tax method results in the same value in use as the post-tax method, because no deferred tax balances arise from the carrying value that is established on a pre-tax basis.

7.62 In practice, it will often be possible to avoid the additional complexities of grossing up to a pre-tax basis. Given that, in principle, the pre-tax cash flows, discounted at a pre-tax rate, should equal the post-tax cash flows discounted at a post-tax rate, it follows that identifying whether or not an asset is impaired can be done more simply at a post-tax level. Companies need to switch into a pre-tax analysis only if an impairment is indicated. FRS 11's example goes on to consider the pre-tax and post-tax relationship when an asset becomes impaired.

Example – FRS 11 introducing impairment

In the above example, the asset has been purchased for £100, but the pre-tax cash flows are now expected to be £60 and not £120 as previously estimated. A tax cash inflow of £12 is now expected, comprising tax on profit before depreciation of £18 (30% of £60) less tax relief on the cost of the asset of £30 (30% of £100). The expected post-tax cash flow is, therefore, £72.

The present value of the post-tax cash flows of £72 (discounted at the post-tax rate of 14%) is £63.2. Thus at a post-tax level there is an impairment loss of £36.8 (that is, £100 less £63.2). Fixed assets, however, are not recognised on a post-tax valuation basis and so the timing difference related to the impairment loss needs to be separately identified and recognised in accordance with SSAP 15.

Since the expected pre-tax cash flow is 50% lower than the previous estimate, the asset's value in use might also be expected to have been reduced by the same margin, that is by £50 from £100 to £50. This would indicate that the balance of post-tax value in use of £13.2 is attributable to the timing difference caused by the impairment loss.

In effect, the tax allowances on the asset that are available to the entity (based on the unimpaired original cost) need to be stripped out of the calculation and replaced by those that would be available if the asset was replaced at its imputed value in use, because the difference represents tax on the timing difference caused by the impairment loss.

It should be noted that if a company has not previously needed to carry out an impairment review, it would not have needed to calculate the pre-tax rate of 20% until now.

The pre-tax value in use (and pre-tax discount rate) can be derived from the known variables which are: the estimated pre-tax cash flows (60); the post-tax market rate of return (14%); the tax rate (30%); and the rate of capital allowance for the cost of the asset (100%). The pre-tax value in use (x) can be derived thus:

x	=	$[60 - 0.3(60 - x)] \times 1/1.14$
x	=	$\dfrac{42 + 0.3x}{1.14}$
1.14x	=	$42 + 0.3x$
0.84x	=	42
x	=	50

The figures in square brackets above consist of two elements. The first is the estimated pre-tax cash flows of 60. The second is the tax cash flows that would arise if the asset were replaced at a cost equal to its impaired value in use (that is, excluding the tax effect of the timing difference caused by the impairment loss). In this calculation, the actual expected tax cash inflow of 12 is substituted by a tax cash flow calculated as $-0.3(60) + 0.3x$, that is a tax cash outflow of 3. This consists of tax of 18 on the pre-tax cash flows of 60 (60 at 30%) less tax relief of 15 on the asset's imputed value in use (50 at 30%).

In this example, the pre-tax discount rate (that is, the rate that discounts the pre-tax cash flows of 60 to the value in use of 50) remains at 20%.

	Cash flows actual expected	Cash flows excluding tax relief on timing difference	Tax relief on timing difference
Pre-tax cash flows	60	60	
Tax cash flows	12	(3)	15
Post-tax cash flows	72	57	15
Pre-tax value in use		50	

Deferred tax is provided on the timing difference that emerges from writing the asset down from its cost of 100 to its value in use of 50. Potentially there is a deferred tax asset of 15 (50 × 30%). Whether or not this deferred tax asset is recognised depends on the application of SSAP 15.

The pre-tax and post-tax figures recognised in the profit and loss account and balance sheet are thus (assuming the deferred tax asset is recognised under SSAP 15):

Profit and loss account	
Pre-tax impairment loss	(50)
Deferred tax (credit)	15
Net loss	(35)
Balance sheet	
Fixed asset	50
Deferred tax asset	15
	65

It should be noted that the balance sheet total of £65 differs from the present value of the post-tax cash flows of £63.2, because the deferred tax balance is not discounted. The present value of the tax cash inflow of £15 receivable in one year's time discounted by 14% is £13.2.

7.63 Although the theory may be understandable, grossing up the net of tax value in use into separate values for the assets concerned and deferred tax balances on the basis required by FRS 11 is likely to be difficult to apply rigidly in practice, since the present value calculations are likely to be multi-period and complex. Given the overall subjectivity of the exercise, suitable approximations should normally be acceptable.

7.64 Some more challenging examples are set out below, to extend the analysis into multi-period cash flows and to draw some practical guidance. These examples illustrate the potential complexity of the 'grossing up' exercise where it is necessary to identify separate pre-tax and deferred tax components of an impairment loss.

Example 1

An entity purchases an asset for 1,000 at the end of year 0. It has an expected useful life of three years. The expected cash flows are shown in schedule 1 and give the entity an expected post-tax rate of return of 7.3%, which is the assumed market rate of return. It has been assumed for simplicity that all cash flows arise at the end of the year.

The assumptions about tax are:

capital allowances – 25% per annum reducing balance
corporation tax – 30%
tax is payable one year in arrears.

The equivalent pre-tax rate is calculated as 9.7%. That is, the rate applied to the pre-tax cash flows of 1,200 which, after tax of 60 has been deducted, gives the required post-tax return of 7.3% on the investment of 1,000.

Schedule 1

	Discount rate %	Present value	Cash flows				
			Year 1	Year 2	Year 3	Year 4	Total
Pre-tax	9.7	1,000	400	400	400		1,200
Tax			75	(64)	(78)	7	(60)
Post-tax	7.3	1,000	475	336	322	7	1,140

The tax cash flows included in schedule 1 are calculated as follows:

	Year 0	Year 1	Year 2	Year 3	Total
Profit	0	(400)	(400)	(400)	(1,200)
Capital allowances	250	187	140	423	1,000
Taxable profit	250	(213)	(260)	23	(200)
Tax payable (30%)	75	(64)	(78)	7	(60)

The relationship between the pre-tax rate of 9.7% and the post-tax rate of 7.3% gives an effective tax rate of 24.7%. This is near to the assumed rate of corporation tax of 30% in this example, but it need not be, as illustrated in schedule 2, where the facts are the same as in schedule 1, except that there is a first year capital allowance of 50% and thereafter 25% reducing balance.

Calculating value in use

The same pre-tax cash flows of 1,200 now give a post-tax rate of return of 8%, because the timing of the tax cash flows is more favourable, whereas the pre-tax rate remains at 9.7%.

Schedule 2

	Discount rate %	Present value	Cash flows				
			Year 1	Year 2	Year 3	Year 4	Total
Pre-tax	9.7	1,000	400	400	400		1,200
Tax			150	(82)	(92)	(36)	(60)
Post-tax	8.0	1,000	550	318	308	(36)	1,140

The tax cash flows included in schedule 2 are calculated as follows:

	Year 0	Year 1	Year 2	Year 3	Total
Profit	0	(400)	(400)	(400)	(1,200)
Capital allowances	500	125	94	28	1,000
Taxable profit	500	(275)	(306)	(119)	(200)
Tax payable (30%)	150	(82)	(92)	(36)	(60)

Example 2 – introducing impairment at year 0

In this example, the tax assumptions are the same as those in schedule 1.

Immediately after the asset was purchased, there was an adverse event that triggered an impairment review. The estimated pre-tax cash flows were revised downwards to 300 per annum. The revised cash flow forecasts are shown in schedule 3.

The present value of the post-tax cash flows is now 812, which includes the benefit of capital allowances on the original cost of 1,000. The asset is clearly impaired. An impaired pre-tax value in use of 750 (that is, a write-down of 25% from the asset's cost of 1,000) would be expected to be a reasonable estimate, since the expected pre-tax cash flows of 900 are 25% lower in

78

aggregate than those previously forecast of 1,200. The present value of the pre-tax cash flows discounted at the original pre-tax rate of 9.7% is indeed 750.

Schedule 3

	Discount rate %	Present value	Cash flows				
			Year 0	Year 1	Year 2	Year 3	Total
Pre-tax	9.7	750	300	300	300		900
Tax			75	(34)	(48)	37	30
Post-tax	7.3	812	375	266	252	37	930

The tax cash flows included in schedule 3 are calculated as follows:

	Year 0	Year 1	Year 2	Year 3	Total
Profit	0	(300)	(300)	(300)	(900)
Capital allowances	250	187	140	423	1,000
Taxable profit	250	(113)	(160)	123	100
Tax payable (30%)	75	(34)	(48)	37	30

The post-tax present value of 812 is the correct post-tax value in use in discounted terms. The exercise that is required is to estimate the pre-tax value in use, the pre-tax discount rate and the deferred tax that arises on the timing difference relating to the impairment loss. (Note that if deferred tax were discounted and provided in full, the impaired carrying value of the fixed asset inclusive of the related deferred tax asset should equal 812).

If the asset were written down from 1,000 to 750, say on a trial and error basis, a timing difference of 250 would arise on the impairment loss. The deferred tax effect at 30% would be a potential asset of 75. The deferred tax asset might not be recognised under SSAP 15, but it needs to be taken into account in the impairment calculations. As the potential carrying value of 825 (impaired asset 750 plus deferred tax 75) exceeds the post-tax value in use of 812, the pre-tax discount rate appears to be too low (and the value in use of 750 too high). However, it should be noted that the deferred tax asset of 75 is not a discounted figure, thus the comparison is not strictly on a like-for-like basis. In practice, a calculation such as this would be acceptable if it gave a reasonable result.

A more sophisticated calculation is shown in Schedule 4. It is the result of an iterative process to find the pre-tax rate and value in use that, when the deferred tax component (that is, the tax benefit relating to the capital allowances still to be obtained on the asset that would not be obtained if the asset were replaced at its impaired value in use) is eliminated from the tax cash flows, approximates the post-tax value in use. This has been done by inserting formulae into the spreadsheet to derive the tax cash flows from the pre-tax value in use and the pre-tax cash flows (using the same assumptions about capital allowances) and adjusting the pre-tax discount rate until the pre-tax value in use equals the post-tax value in use. In this iterative calculation, the pre-tax value in use, the tax cash flows and the pre-tax discount rate are not known in advance.

The calculation gives a value in use of 750 and a pre-tax discount rate of 9.7%, as expected. The total tax cash outflows of 45 in this calculation represent tax at 30% on the future pre-tax profits of 150 after post-impairment depreciation (that is, cash flows of 900 less the impaired carrying value of 750).

Schedule 4

	Discount rate %	Present value	Cash flows				
			Year 1	Year 2	Year 3	Year 4	Total
Pre-tax	9.7	750	300	300	300		900
Tax			56	(48)	(58)	5	(45)
Post-tax	7.3	750	356	252	242	5	855

The tax cash flows can be proved by calculating capital allowances on the impaired asset value of 750 as follows:

	Year 0	Year 1	Year 2	Year 3	Total
Profit	0	(300)	(300)	(300)	(900)
Capital allowances	187	140	106	317	750
Taxable profit	187	(160)	(194)	17	(150)
Tax payable (30%)	56	(48)	(58)	5	(45)

Schedule 5 demonstrates that the *present value* of the deferred tax asset of 75 discounted at the post-tax rate of 7.3% is 62. It compares the tax cash flows in Schedule 3 where the entity has claimed capital allowances on the original cost of 1,000 with the tax cash flows in Schedule 4 where the entity has claimed capital allowances on the impaired carrying value of 750. The difference between the two cash flows represents the timing difference caused by the impairment loss. This timing difference of 75 is recognised as a deferred tax asset if permitted by SSAP 15.

Schedule 5

	Discount rate %	Present value	Tax cash flows				
			Year 1	Year 2	Year 3	Year 4	Total
Schedule 3	7.3	29	75	(34)	(48)	37	30
Schedule 4	7.3	(33)	56	(48)	(58)	5	(45)
Difference	7.3	62	19	14	10	32	75

Furthermore, adding the present value of 62 (instead of 75) to the value in use of 750 gives a post-tax value in use to the entity of 812, which is the post-tax value in use that was originally calculated in schedule 3.

Therefore, 750 is the correct impaired carrying value and 9.7% is the correct pre-tax discount rate.

It should be noted that in the above calculations, the pre-tax rate of 9.7% was derived from the post-tax rate of 7.3% and did not have to be known.

The effect of the above calculation on the financial statements, assuming the deferred tax is recognised under SSAP 15 is as follows:

Profit and loss account	
Pre-tax impairment loss	(250)
Deferred tax asset (30% of 250)	75
Net loss	(175)
Balance sheet	
Fixed asset (1,000 – 250)	750
Deferred tax asset*	75
	825
* Under SSAP 15, the deferred tax asset might not be recognised	

Example 3 – introducing impairment during the asset's life

The initial cash flow estimates are the same as in schedule 1. The cash flows in year 1 are in line with plan, but there is an indicator of impairment at the end of year 1 and revised cash flow projections are prepared as in schedule 6.

The balance sheet carrying values relating to the asset at the end of year 1 (assuming straight-line depreciation over 3 years) are:

Asset carrying value (1,000 – 333)	667
Deferred tax liability*	(31)
Corporation tax on year 1 cash flows	(64)
	572
* Comprises deferred tax on a timing difference of 104 at 30%. The timing difference of 104 comprises the book value of 667 less tax written down value of 563 (cost of 1,000 less capital allowances of 250 in year 0 and 187 in year 1).	

The post-tax value in use is only 404, so clearly the asset is impaired (that is, compared with the post-tax balance sheet carrying value of 572). The pre-tax value in use can be estimated by varying the discount rate and estimating the deferred tax effect of the resulting impairment loss and comparing the result with the post-tax value in use. For example, the previously calculated pre-tax rate of 9.7% gives a value in use of 436 and an impairment loss of 231 (that is, 667 less 436).

Schedule 6

	Discount rate %	Present value	Cash flows			
			Year 2	Year 3	Year 4	Total
Pre-tax	9.7	436	250	250	0	500
Tax			(64)	(33)	52	(45)
Post-tax	7.3	404	186	217	52	455

The tax cash flows in schedule 6 are calculated as follows:

	Year 1	Year 2	Year 3	Total
Profit	(400)	(250)	(250)	(900)
Capital allowances	187	140	423	750
Taxable profit	(213)	(110)	173	(150)
Tax payable (30%)	(64)	(33)	52	(45)

If the asset were written down to 436, a timing difference of 231 would arise (667 less 436). The deferred tax effect of this timing difference at 30% is 69. The balance sheet amounts relating to the asset would be:

Asset carrying value	436
Deferred tax asset*	38
Corporation tax on year 1 cash flows	(64)
	410

* Deferred tax liability of 31 brought forward, less deferred tax credit of 69 relating to impairment loss.

This might be determined to be a reasonable estimate, as it is not significantly different from the post-tax value in use of 404. Of course, this method of estimation is only a broad approximation because, whereas the value in use is a discounted valuation, the other components (deferred tax and corporation tax payable) are not.

A more sophisticated calculation is shown in schedule 7, which is similar to the calculation in schedule 4.

The calculation is the result of an iterative process to find the pre-tax rate and value in use that, when the deferred tax component (that is, the tax benefit relating to the capital allowances still to be obtained on the asset that would not be obtained if the asset were replaced at its impaired value in use) of the impairment loss is eliminated from the tax cash flows, approximates to the post-tax value in use. This has been done by inserting formulae into the spreadsheet to derive the tax cash flows from the pre-tax value in use and the pre-tax cash flows (assuming the normal capital allowances were available, that is 25% on value in use for years 2 and 3 and a balancing allowance receivable in year 4) and adjusting the pre-tax discount rate until the pre-tax value in use equals the post-tax value in use. In this iterative calculation, the pre-tax value in use, the tax cash flows and the pre-tax discount rate are not known in advance. The calculation gives a value in use of 436 and a pre-tax discount rate of 9.7%.

The total tax payable of 19 in this calculation represents tax at 30% on the future pre-tax profits of 64 after post-impairment depreciation (that is, cash flows of 500 less impaired carrying value 436).

Schedule 7

	Discount rate %	Present value	Cash flows			
			Year 2	Year 3	Year 4	Total
Pre-tax	9.7	436	250	250	0	500
Tax			32	(50)	(1)	(19)
Post-tax	7.3	436	282	200	(1)	481

The tax cash flows can be proved by calculating capital allowances on the impaired asset value of 436 as follows:

	Year 2	Year 3	Year 4	Total
Profit	0	(250)	(250)	(500)
Capital allowances	109	82	245	436
Taxable profit	109	(168)	(5)	(64)
Tax payable (30%)	32	(50)	(1)	(19)

The effect of the above calculation on the financial statements in year 1, assuming the deferred tax asset is recognised under SSAP 15, is as follows:

Profit and loss account	
Pre-tax impairment loss	(231)
Deferred tax credit (30% of 231)	69
Net loss	(162)
Balance sheet	
Fixed asset (667 − 231)	436
Deferred tax asset*	38
	474
* Under SSAP 15, the deferred tax asset might not be recognised.	

7.65 The above examples illustrate the complexities involved in deriving a true pre-tax discount rate from a post-tax rate of return where the latter (such as an entity's WACC) is the key observable market rate of return that is available to an entity. There are some practical ways of simplifying the exercise which, in many cases, would give a reasonable basis for identifying material impairment losses and would produce reasonable estimates of pre-tax impairment losses.

7.66 If entities usually prepare discounted cash flow forecasts on a post-tax basis, such calculations should normally identify whether or not a material impairment in an IGU's carrying value has occurred. If no impairment is identified, there is no need to switch into a pre-tax analysis.

7.67 Where an impairment is identified at a post-tax level, a pre-tax analysis is required to identify the pre-tax discount rate (which is required to be disclosed in the financial statements) and the asset or IGU's pre-tax value in use from which the pre-tax impairment loss and the related deferred tax effects are derived.

7.68 In practice, entities are likely to find it simpler to estimate the pre-tax discount rate (which could be viewed as the pre-tax rate of return that the entity would use in making an investment decision) instead of carrying out the iterative calculations that are illustrated in the above examples. As a starting point, the pre-tax rate could be estimated by 'grossing up' the post-tax rate to reflect the effective rate of corporation tax applicable to the operating profits of the IGU being reviewed. If necessary, the estimated pre-tax rate should be varied to reflect the effect of special factors that might materially distort the relationship between the post-tax rate and the pre-tax rate - for example, where the timing of the tax cash flows is very favourable to the entity because of accelerated capital allowances, the 'grossing up' rate would be expected to be less than the effective rate (see schedule 2 in example 1 above). Discounting the pre-tax cash flows by that estimated pre-tax discount rate would result in an estimated value in use (and an estimated impairment loss) of the asset or IGU. Such a method of calculating value in use would need to be reviewed for reasonableness, but should often be adequate, since the impairment calculations as a whole, being as they are based on best estimates of unknown future events, generally provide fairly broad measures of material impairment losses.

7.69 Having estimated an impairment loss on a pre-tax basis, the deferred tax effect can be simply calculated by applying the current tax rate to the impairment loss. The resulting deferred tax asset should be recognised in accordance with SSAP 15.

Chapter 8

Recognition of impairment losses

Allocation of impairment losses to assets of income-generating units

8.1   Where the recoverable amounts of fixed assets can be estimated individually, the recognition of impairment losses is straightforward. The assets are written down to their individual recoverable amounts (that is, the higher of net realisable value and value in use).

8.2   Where the recoverable amounts of fixed assets or goodwill cannot be estimated individually and, hence, they need to be estimated in aggregate for the IGUs to which they belong, the question arises as to which assets in the IGU should be written down where the carrying value of an IGU's net assets in aggregate exceeds its recoverable amount.

8.3   FRS 11 requires that, unless an impairment is obviously attributable to a specific asset in an IGU, an impairment loss attributable to an IGU should be allocated to write down the assets in the following order:

■   Purchased goodwill.
■   Capitalised intangibles.
■   Tangible assets, on a *pro rata* or more appropriate basis.
[FRS 11 para 48].

The reason for this hierarchy is to ensure that the assets with the most subjective valuations are written off first.

Example

An IGU has attributed net assets of £500m, as set out in the table below. An impairment review estimates the present value of its future cash flows to be £300m. There is an impairment loss of £200m which is written off as shown.

	£m	Write-off £m
Purchased goodwill	150	(150)
Intangible assets	30	(30)
Net tangible assets	320	(20)
Net assets	500	(200)
Value in use	300	

8.4   However, within this allocation framework no intangible asset with a readily ascertainable market value or tangible asset with a net realisable value that can be measured reliably should be written down below those values. [FRS 11 para 49]. It should be noted that very few intangible assets have a readily ascertainable market value as defined in the FRS.

8.5   This rule accords with the general principle in the FRS that an asset should not be written down below the higher of its net realisable value or value in use. Whilst the value in use of individual assets in an IGU may not be determinable, their net realisable values may be. For example, individual properties occupied by branches of an integrated financial services operation that is treated as a single IGU for calculating value in use may have determinable market values. Any impairment losses that cannot be allocated on a pro-rata basis to specific assets because they have higher net realisable values are allocated to other assets in the IGU.

8.6   The allocation process is important because it establishes new carrying values for individual assets that form the basis for subsequent depreciation charges and for accounting for subsequent disposals. However, it is necessarily arbitrary. The allocation between tangible fixed assets in an IGU would normally be made *pro rata* to their individual carrying values. However, management has discretion to adopt a different basis if that is considered to be more appropriate.

Example

The carrying value of an IGU's assets is £130 in aggregate, comprising tangible assets as analysed in the table below. The IGU's property has a market value of £70; the other assets do not have determinable net realisable values. The IGU's value in use is estimated to be £100, resulting in an impairment loss of £30 to be allocated.

The impairment loss is allocated to the assets of the IGU based on their relative carrying values, except that the property is not written down below its net realisable value of £70. Part of the loss that would otherwise be allocated to the property is reallocated to the other fixed assets, as illustrated below.

	Carrying value before impairment review	Impairment loss allocation		Impaired carrying value
		Pro-rata	Reallocated	
Property	80	18	10	70
Plant & equipment	30	7	12	18
Fixtures & fittings	20	5	8	12
	130	30	30	100

Different methods of treating goodwill

8.7 Chapter 6 explains the principles for allocating purchased goodwill to IGUs. Two methods are permitted and these are to some extent optional.

8.8   The first method is to fully allocate purchased goodwill to individual IGUs (suggested methods of allocating goodwill are discussed in chapter 6). Where relevant, the carrying values of IGUs reviewed for impairment then include a share of purchased goodwill.

8.9   The second method allows the purchased goodwill component to be reviewed for impairment at a higher level of aggregation than other assets. IGUs may be combined for testing the recoverability of the related goodwill if:

■   they were acquired as part of the same investment; and
■   they are involved in similar parts of the business.
[FRS 11 para 34]

8.10   If the second method is adopted, a two-tier impairment review is required, comprising:

■   A review at the individual IGU level, where the assets and liabilities (excluding any allocation of goodwill) are reviewed for impairment. Any impairment loss is attributed to the IGU's assets.

■   A review at a higher level to test the recoverability of the goodwill, where all the IGUs to which the goodwill relates are reviewed in aggregate. This review compares the carrying amount of the net assets of those IGUs and the purchased goodwill in aggregate with their combined value in use. Any further impairment loss identified at this level relates to the goodwill.

Example

An acquisition made some years ago comprised two IGUs, A and B. There has been an indicator that the carrying value of A may be impaired.

A – Recognition of impairment where goodwill is allocated

The carrying values of the net assets and goodwill of IGUs A and B, and their value in use, are determined as follows:

Income-generating unit	A £m	B £m	Total £m
Net assets	220	110	330
Goodwill	40	40	80
Total net assets	260	150	410
Value in use	200	180	380
Impairment	60		

In this example, where purchased goodwill is allocated to the separate IGUs there is an impairment loss of £60m in A, reducing the carrying value of its net assets and goodwill to £200m. The impairment loss is attributed £40m to goodwill and £20m to other fixed assets.

The carrying values after recognising the impairment loss are as follows.

Carrying values after impairment	A £m	B £m	Total £m
Net assets	200	110	310
Goodwill	–	40	40
Total net assets	200	150	350

B – Recognition of impairment where goodwill is aggregated

If A and B, which were acquired together in one investment, were involved in similar parts of the business, the calculations could be done as follows:

Income-generating unit	A £m	B £m	Goodwill £m	Total £m
Net assets	220	110	80	410
Value in use	200	180		380
Impairment	20		10	30

First, IGU A is reviewed for impairment without any allocation of goodwill. The value in use of £200m is compared with the carrying value of its net assets (excluding goodwill) of £220m. There is an impairment loss of £20m, reducing the carrying value of its net assets to £200m.

Secondly, A and B may be combined to assess the recoverability of the goodwill. The value in use of the combined units is now £380m, which is compared with the aggregate carrying value of the net assets and goodwill, which is £390m (that is, £410m less the £20m written off the net assets of unit A). Therefore, a further impairment loss of £10m is recognised to write down the goodwill to £70m.

The carrying values after recognising the impairment loss are as follows.

Carrying values after impairment	A £m	B £m	Goodwill £m	Total £m
Net assets	200	110	70	380

8.11 The above example illustrates that significantly different accounting results can be achieved by adopting different approaches to aggregation and also serves to place impairment testing in its context – showing that impairment tests are not exact mathematical exercises. Under the first method, where no aggregation assumed, there is an impairment loss of £60 million. Under the second method, where goodwill is reviewed on an aggregate basis, there is an impairment loss of only £30 million. The second method in effect allows the impairment in the value of the goodwill of the impaired IGU to be partly offset against an increase in the value of the goodwill of the unimpaired IGU since its acquisition.

It should be noted that this offset would not be allowed if A and B were involved in dissimilar activities or were acquired in different acquisitions.

8.12 It should also be noted that if A or B were subsequently sold separately, an allocation of the carrying value of goodwill would be necessary to eliminate it from the balance sheet (that is, to write it off as part of the profit or loss on disposal). Where the first method (allocating goodwill to separate IGUs) has been used to account for impairment, this is straightforward. Where the second method has been used, the allocation of goodwill between A and B that previously was not made would have to be made if there is a sale. In the above example, if A were sold, a loss of £30 million would have to be recognised on disposal in respect of purchased goodwill attributable to A that has not previously been written off. The figure of £30 million reflects the purchased goodwill of £40 million that would have originally been allocated to A less the previous impairment of £10 million that would have been attributable to A.

Central assets

8.13 Central assets that provide benefits to two or more IGUs in an enterprise (such as corporate head offices, computer centres or research facilities) should be dealt with in one of two ways.

- First, if possible, their carrying values should be apportioned across the IGUs that they support on a logical and systematic basis. The resulting carrying values of each IGU are then compared with their recoverable amounts.

- Secondly, if it is not possible to apportion central assets meaningfully, they are covered in a two-tier impairment review. The methodology for the two-tier review is similar to that relating to goodwill and permits the central assets to be reviewed in aggregate with all the IGUs that they support.

8.14   However, the two methods are not strictly optional as they may be in some circumstances for goodwill – if central assets can be allocated meaningfully across IGUs, they should be (see chapter 6 for further discussion of allocation methodology).

8.15   As with goodwill, the two methods of dealing with central assets may give different overall impairment results. The 'two-tier' approach could avoid some impairment losses that would be identified in the full allocation approach. The recoverable amount of one IGU might only just exceed the carrying value of its operating assets (without any allocation of central assets), whereas the recoverable amounts of the other IGUs might exceed the carrying values of both their operating assets and the central assets. In such circumstances, the 'two tier' review would not reveal any impairment, whereas the full allocation approach would reveal an impairment in the marginally profitable IGU. The 'two-tier' approach has the effect of allowing central assets to be allocated first to the more profitable IGUs, thus protecting less profitable IGUs from impairment losses. The view would presumably be that the central assets are not impaired as long as the more profitable parts of the business can support their carrying values.

8.16   The following examples illustrate the full allocation and two-tier approaches to dealing with central assets, coupled with the different approaches to the allocation of goodwill.

Example 1 – full allocation of central assets and goodwill to individual IGUs

An entity comprises two IGUs, A and B. The entity has a head office with a book value of £30m.

The following table illustrates the impairment review based on the calculation of value in use assuming that both the head office and purchased goodwill are allocated fully to the two IGUs. The head office is allocated *pro rata* to the other net assets; thus, £20m is allocated to A and £10m is allocated to B. (Note that any intra-group cash flows relating to the use of the head office should be excluded from the IGUs' value in use calculations in order to avoid double-counting).

Income-generating unit	A £m	B £m	Total £m
Directly attributable net assets	220	110	330
Head office	20	10	30
Goodwill	40	40	80
Total net assets	280	160	440
Value in use	200	180	380
Impairment	80		80
Net assets as written down	200	160	360

There is an impairment loss of £80m in A. This needs to be allocated between the assets of A – first to the allocated goodwill and thereafter to the tangible fixed assets. Possible methods are illustrated in the following table.

The first method allocates the balance of the impairment loss after goodwill write-off (£40m) *pro-rata* between all the tangible fixed assets attributable to the IGU, including the head office allocation. (The impairment attributable to the head office and the IGU's tangible fixed assets is calculated as 40 × 20/240 and 40 × 220/240 respectively.) The rationale would be that the part of the head office that is dedicated to the unprofitable IGU is impaired.

Some may find it curious to write down a proportion of the head office in this way and may prefer to charge the whole impairment loss against the IGU's operating assets, as in the second method. But it is still necessary (if possible) to allocate the head office asset for the purpose of the impairment calculations, even if impairment losses arising are allocated only to the IGU's assets.

Allocation of impairment loss	1 £m	2 £m
Goodwill	40.0	40.0
Head office	3.3	-
Directly attributable tangible fixed assets of A	36.7	40.0
	80.0	80.0

A further complication that could arise is where the head office had a market value in excess of its impaired value as calculated on a value in use basis – say, its net realisable value were in excess of £30m. In that situation, because no asset can be written down below its net realisable value, the whole of the impairment loss would have to be allocated to the IGU's tangible fixed assets.

Example 2 – full allocation of central assets; goodwill reviewed in aggregate

The facts are as in example 1. The following table illustrates the impairment review assuming that the head office is allocated to the two IGUs, but goodwill is reviewed in aggregate, because it relates to a single acquisition and the two IGUs are involved in similar parts of the business.

The allocated net assets of A are impaired by £40m and the capitalised goodwill in aggregate is impaired by £20m, giving a total impairment loss of only £60m.

Income-generating unit	A £m	B £m	Goodwill £m	Total £m
Directly attributable net assets	220	110	80	410
Head office	20	10	–	30
Total net assets	240	120	80	440
Value in use	200	180		380
Impairment	40		20	60
Net assets as written down	200	120	60	380

This method in effect allows the impairment of goodwill that was recognised in example 1 (£40m) to be offset by unrecognised internally generated goodwill of £20m in unit B. This offset would not be allowed if A and B were involved in dissimilar activities.

The impairment loss of £40m attributable to IGU A would be allocated on one of the bases described in example 1. Method 1 is a *pro rata* allocation between the IGU's tangible fixed assets and the allocated portion of the head office; method 2 allocates the whole of the impairment loss after goodwill write-off to the IGU's directly attributable fixed assets.

Allocation of impairment loss	1 £m	2 £m
Goodwill	20.0	20.0
Head office	3.3	–
Directly attributable tangible fixed assets of A	36.7	40.0
	60.0	60.0

Example 3 – two-tier review of central assets and goodwill

The facts are the same as in examples 1 and 2. The following table illustrates the impairment review if neither the head office nor purchased goodwill is allocated to the individual IGUs. Instead, two impairment reviews are carried out. The first review is at the individual IGU level, comparing value in use with the carrying value of the net assets directly involved in the businesses (that is, excluding central assets and goodwill). The second review brings in the head office and goodwill at an aggregate level.

The first review shows an impairment loss of £20m in IGU A.

The second review compares the aggregate value in use (£380m) with the aggregate net asset value recognised after the first impairment review (£420m), comprising the impaired net assets of unit A (£200m), the net assets of unit B (£110m), the head office (£30m) and the capitalised goodwill (£80m). This results in a further impairment loss of £40m, which is allocated to the goodwill.

Income-generating unit	A £m	B £m	Head office £m	Goodwill £m	Total £m
Directly attributable net assets	220	110	30	80	440
Value in use	200	180			380
Impairment	20			40	60
Net assets as written down	200	110	30	40	380

The impairment loss of £20m attributable to IGU A would be allocated *pro-rata* to its tangible fixed assets. The overall impairment loss would be allocated as follows.

Allocation of impairment loss	£m
Goodwill	40
Head office	-
Directly attributable tangible fixed assets of A	20
	60

8.17 The three examples above illustrate how different approaches to allocating central assets and goodwill can result in either different impairment losses or different allocations of impairment losses as between operating assets, central assets and goodwill. A further issue is to ensure that cash flows relating to central overheads are treated consistently in the calculation of value in use, that is, that they are neither omitted from nor double-counted in the impairment review. For example, in example 3 above, where no allocation of the head office carrying value was made to the IGUs, the inclusion of any compensating cash outflows relating to the head office property in the calculation of the IGUs' value in use would also affect the impairment calculations. Thus any rent payable to the parent company in relation to the head office would reduce the IGUs' value in use and, as a result, any impairment losses attributable to the

IGUs would be correspondingly increased. The message is that the calculations can be significantly affected by subjective allocations of central assets or central costs.

Integration of acquired businesses with existing operations

8.18 FRS 11 addresses a specific issue relating to purchased goodwill. The situation is where an acquired business that resulted in the recognition of purchased goodwill is integrated with other operations of the acquiring group and, as a result, loses its separate identity.

8.19 Where operations are merged in this way, the assets and purchased goodwill of the acquired business may then form part of the carrying value of a larger IGU that includes assets of pre-existing operations. If an impairment review of the larger IGU is required, its value in use would be compared with its carrying value. The IGU's carrying value comprises the carrying values of the recognised net assets of the acquired and pre-existing operations, together with the carrying value of the purchased goodwill relating to the acquired business. The IGU's value in use will reflect the value of any internally generated goodwill in the existing business, which is not permitted to be recognised as an asset. If impairment reviews were carried out on this basis, an impairment relating to the acquired business could be avoided to the extent that it was offset by unrecognised internally generated goodwill in the existing business with which the acquired business was merged.

8.20 FRS 11 sets out a method that should be applied to a combined IGU that contains both (capitalised) purchased goodwill relating to the acquired business and (unrecognised) internally generated goodwill that relates to the existing business. This method notionally preserves a distinction between the two types of goodwill in the IGU, and requires impairment losses to be allocated between them in order to prevent a potential impairment of the purchased goodwill from being avoided.

8.21 FRS 11 requires the internally generated goodwill of the existing business to be estimated at the date of merging the businesses. This exercise requires the existing business to be valued separately before the integration (that is, its value in use should be estimated). The internally generated goodwill should be calculated by deducting the fair value of the net assets (and any purchased goodwill) of the existing business from its estimated value in use before combining the businesses. [FRS 11 paras 50 to 52].

8.22 The internally generated goodwill as calculated should be added to the carrying value of the net assets of the combined IGU for the purpose of the impairment review as illustrated below (note that the internally generated goodwill is not actually recognised in the financial statements). The internally generated goodwill is assumed to be amortised on the same basis as the purchased goodwill.

Notional carrying value of integrated income-generating unit		
	Net assets	**Goodwill**
New acquisition	Fair value	Purchased
Existing business	Carrying value*	Internally generated
		Purchased (re previous acquisitions by the existing business, if any)
* that is, existing book value, but note that fair values are used to calculate the internally generated goodwill when the businesses are integrated		

8.23 FRS 11 states that this exercise should be carried out whenever an acquisition that gives rise to goodwill is merged with an existing business. [FRS 11 para 52]. Even if a full-scale impairment review is not required (say, because there is no indicator that the carrying amounts of fixed assets or goodwill may not be recoverable), the calculations are still necessary to create the records that would be required to carry out a full impairment review later if, say, an indicator of impairment arose some years after the integration of businesses.

8.24 At the time when the businesses are integrated, if the aggregate carrying value of the net assets and goodwill, including the notional internally generated goodwill as illustrated above, exceeds the recoverable amount of the combined IGU, the impairment should be allocated wholly to the capitalised purchased goodwill relating to the acquired business and, hence, recognised in full in the consolidated profit and loss account. This is because any impairment of the existing business will have been identified and recognised when the exercise to calculate the internally generated goodwill of the existing business (that is, when calculating fair values of the net assets) was carried out. By definition, therefore, if a further impairment arises when the review of the combined business is carried out, it must relate to the purchased goodwill of the acquired business. This should ensure that any overpayment for the acquisition is identified and written off and is not offset against the unrecognised goodwill of the existing business.

8.25 Any goodwill impairments identified in subsequent years should be apportioned on a *pro rata* basis between the carrying value of the purchased goodwill and the notional carrying value of the internally generated goodwill. Only the impairment allocated to the capitalised purchased goodwill would be charged in the profit and loss account.

Example

The combined balance sheet of an IGU formed by integrating an acquired business with an existing business is set out in the following table. The figures in italics are those that include the notional value of (unrecognised) internally generated goodwill in the existing business.

The actual recognised net assets and purchased goodwill of the combined IGU amounts to £400m. Added to this is unrecognised internally generated goodwill in the existing business of £500m (which derives from the value that was estimated when the businesses were merged, after deducting notional amortisation since that date), making a notional total of £900m.

Impairment review of combined IGU			
	Acquisition	Existing business	Combined
Net assets	80	100	180
Goodwill	220	*500*	*720*
Total	300	*600*	*900*
Value in use			750
Impairment	46	*104*	*150*

An impairment review of the combined IGU compares its value in use of £750m with its aggregate (notional) net assets of £900m.

Assuming that this impairment review takes place some years after the integration of the acquired business, the impairment loss of £150m is allocated *pro rata* between the purchased goodwill (acquisition) and the internally generated goodwill (existing business). This allocates £46m to the former and £104m to the latter.

Only the impairment loss of £46m allocated to the capitalised purchased goodwill is written off in the consolidated profit and loss account.

If, however, the impairment was identified when the businesses were integrated, the whole loss of £150m would be allocated to the capitalised purchased goodwill relating to the acquisition and, hence, written off in the consolidated profit and loss account (see para 8.24).

It should be noted that if this *pro rata* exercise were not required, in the above example no impairment loss would be recognised in the profit and loss account. That is because there would be no impairment of the combined IGUs' recognised net assets and purchased goodwill, which amount only to £400m. The impairment of the goodwill in the acquired business would in effect be offset against the unrecognised internally generated goodwill (£500m) in the existing business. Hence, the recoverable amount of the combined IGU would have to fall below £400m before any impairment loss were recognised in the consolidated profit and loss account.

8.26 This is a complicated approach and somewhat artificial. It was developed alongside the new rules for capitalising and amortising purchased goodwill in FRS 10 and appears to be a consequence of the possibility of carrying goodwill permanently as an asset or amortising it over very long periods (more than 20 years). FRS 10 requires such long-life purchased goodwill balances to be reviewed annually for impairment in order to demonstrate formally that they are recoverable. The ability to perform annual impairment reviews on purchased goodwill balances is a pre-condition for rebutting FRS 10's presumption that goodwill should be amortised against profits over a period of no more than 20 years. Unless there was some standardised basis for measuring the recoverable amount of purchased goodwill in situations where the acquired business had lost its separate identity through the merging of operations, it might appear that it would not be possible to carry out an impairment review on the capitalised goodwill relating to the original acquisition. Groups that subsumed their acquisitions would then be less likely to be in a position to rebut FRS 10's presumption that the useful economic life does not exceed 20 years than those groups that ran their acquisitions as stand-alone businesses.

Goodwill previously written off to reserves

8.27 A further complication arises where the balance sheet of the existing business includes some purchased goodwill that was previously written off to reserves before capitalisation of purchased goodwill became mandatory and remains written off as permitted by the transitional provisions of FRS 10. Such goodwill is not internally generated goodwill of the existing business and so it should be treated in the impairment calculations as purchased goodwill within the existing business. This would mean that the notional balance sheet created for the purpose of allocating impairment losses would include three elements in respect of goodwill: purchased goodwill that has been capitalised; purchased goodwill that has been written off to reserves; and notional internally generated goodwill.

8.28   When it comes to allocating impairment losses to goodwill, it would seem logical to allocate the impairment *pro rata* to these three elements. The impairment relating to the element of goodwill remaining in reserves may or may not be recognised in the profit and loss account at that time (in addition to the impairment attributed to the capitalised purchased goodwill), depending on the group's policy for recognising such impairments. If the group's policy is not to account for goodwill written off to reserves until the business is disposed of, then no impairment relating to that goodwill would be recognised until disposal, when all the attributable goodwill that has not previously been written off in the profit and loss account would be written off as part of the profit or loss on disposal.

Impairment and depreciation

8.29   When a fixed asset or purchased goodwill has been impaired, the remaining carrying value (if any) should be amortised over the remaining useful economic life. The remaining useful economic life and, where applicable, estimated residual value, should also be reviewed and, if necessary, revised. [FRS 11 para 21]. (Note that FRS 10 does not permit any residual value to be assigned to goodwill.)

8.30   This requirement reiterates the normal principle in accounting for fixed assets that asset lives and residual values should be regularly reviewed to ensure they are realistic and be revised if this is not the case in the light of experience or changed circumstances. An impairment warrants particular attention, because it may indicate that previously estimated asset lives are unrealistically long and may need to be shortened.

Assets held for disposal

8.31   If a decision is made to sell an asset, a practical issue is when should the expected sale proceeds be factored into the value in use calculation in place of the cash flows from continued use. This may affect the timing and measurement of any impairment losses.

8.32 FRS 11 para 31 states: *"The income stream of a fixed asset to be disposed of will be largely independent of the income stream of other assets. Such an asset therefore forms an income-generating unit of its own and does not belong to any other income-generating unit."* This suggests that the measurement of recoverable amount would normally anticipate the disposal when it is formally factored into management's cash flow projections. Value in use (which includes the estimated cash flows from the asset's ultimate disposal) would then be similar to net realisable value; hence, the future cash flows of the IGU to which the asset may have formerly belonged are no longer taken into account.

8.33 Similarly, where a decision is made to sell or terminate a business, the amounts expected to be recoverable from the sale or closure of the business would then provide the basis for measuring the recoverable amount of its fixed assets and goodwill. In the case of a business for sale, if the carrying values of the net assets and capitalised goodwill exceeded in aggregate their recoverable amount (which would be based on the expected sale proceeds), the assets are impaired.

8.34 It is also useful to consider how the requirements of FRS 11 interact with FRS 3 and FRS 12 where losses are expected to be incurred in respect of disposals of fixed assets or businesses. FRS 3 and FRS 12 prohibit recognition of provisions for liabilities in respect of sales or terminations of businesses until (a) in the case of a sale, there is a binding sale agreement, or (b) in the case of a termination, a constructive obligation has been incurred (requiring a detailed formal plan and evidence that implementation has started or that the plan has been communicated to those affected).

8.35 Provisions do not include amounts written off assets. The expression that is sometimes used 'provision for loss on disposal of fixed assets' is not a provision in the sense of FRS 12 and any such loss should not be shown as a provision or liability. Both FRS 3 (para 45) and FRS 12 (para 84) refer to the need for asset values to be reviewed for impairment before any provisions are recognised. For example, FRS 3 states that where a decision has been made to sell an operation, but there is no binding contract or other demonstrable commitment to the sale at the reporting date, no provisions for future costs or losses should be made but any impairments (formerly permanent diminutions) in asset values should be recorded.

8.36   Thus impairment losses should be recognised as soon as a disposal is envisaged, if they have not been identified and recognised earlier. The following example illustrates the accounting for the sale of an operation that takes place after the year end.

Example

A group decides before the year end to sell a subsidiary. The sale will take place after the year end and after the financial statements of the group are signed. The carrying values of the subsidiary's fixed assets and purchased goodwill at the year end are £300,000 and £100,000 respectively. Working capital is assumed to be zero.

The subsidiary makes a loss of £110,000 before depreciation from the year end to the date the financial statements are signed. Further losses up to the date of sale are estimated to be £20,000. The group is negotiating the sale at the time of signing the financial statements and expects the proceeds on sale will be £150,000. It is assumed that the group does not fund the subsidiary's losses after the balance sheet date

As mentioned above, where there is no binding sale agreement, no provision for loss on sale should be made, but the value of the subsidiary's net assets consolidated will still have to be considered to determine whether an impairment loss needs to be recognised. If no impairment losses were recognised in respect of the fixed assets and goodwill amounting to £400,000, the group would expect to incur losses of £250,000 in the subsequent year, comprising the subsidiary's expected future losses of £130,000 and an estimated loss on sale of £120,000, as illustrated below:

	£'000	£'000
Fixed assets		300
Goodwill		100
Assets to be reviewed for impairment		400
Loss up to date of sale	(110)	
	(20)	(130)
Estimated net assets at date of sale		270
Expected proceeds on sale		150
Estimated loss on sale		(120)

It is clear in this example that the subsidiary's assets are impaired, because their carrying values are not recoverable. The subsidiary's net assets and goodwill would form a separate IGU, because the subsidiary is to be disposed of. The recoverable amount is £150,000, which is the cash inflow expected from ultimate disposal and represents the subsidiary's value in use to the group (discounting has been ignored for simplicity). It is assumed that net realisable value at the balance sheet date would be similar.

The impairment loss is, therefore, £250,000, which would be allocated first to write-off the goodwill of £100,000 and secondly to write down the subsidiary's fixed assets by the balance of £150,000. The impairment loss of £250,000 is the same amount that might have been provided for as a provision for loss on disposal had there been a binding sale agreement at the balance sheet date.

After the impairment loss of £250,000 has been recognised, the amounts to be included in the group's profit and loss account in the subsequent year in respect of the subsidiary would be:

	£'000
Operating losses	(130)
Profit on disposal	130
Net profit or loss	nil

The profit on disposal is calculated as follows:

	£'000
Fixed assets (as impaired)	150
Goodwill	nil
	150
Operating losses	(130)
Net assets at date of sale	20
Proceeds on sale	150
Profit on sale	130

8.37 The above example demonstrates that, whereas FRS 3 and FRS 12 restrict the circumstances where provisions for losses on sale can be recognised, FRS 11 has increased the emphasis on recognising impairments of assets at an earlier point in time. Issues concerning the presentation of such losses in the profit and loss account – whether the loss should be treated as an impairment (charged against operating profit) or as a loss on sale (charged as a non-operating exceptional item) are considered in chapter 10.

Corporate structures – issues for parent companies and subsidiaries

Parent's investment in subsidiaries

8.38 Where capitalised goodwill on consolidation is written down as a result of impairment, the carrying value of the parent company's investment in the relevant subsidiary should also be reviewed for impairment. [FRS 10 para 42].

8.39 The recoverable amount (if determined by value in use) of an investment in a subsidiary would normally be based on the present value of the subsidiary's estimated cash flows.

8.40 The goodwill and other net assets in the consolidated financial statements that are attributable to an impaired subsidiary will usually differ from the subsidiary's carrying value in the parent's balance sheet as time goes by after the acquisition. The likelihood that the parent's investment has also been impaired will depend partly on its accounting policy, which may be:

- Cost less provision for impairment.
- Cost (excluding share premium qualifying for merger relief or group reconstruction relief) less provision for impairment.
- Net asset value (including unamortised goodwill).

Subsidiaries that are part of larger IGUs

8.41 For groups, FRS 11 is principally targeted at identifying and recognising impairment losses from a group perspective. Thus the whole group as a reporting entity is divided into separate IGUs for the purpose of impairment reviews, such that the IGUs in aggregate cover the whole group and are non-overlapping.

8.42 Individual subsidiaries may also be separate reporting entities, but the allocation of a group's activities between separate companies within a group does not necessarily coincide with the way the group's IGUs are defined.

8.43 Issues arise where a subsidiary's activities form part of a larger IGU in the group. In particular, the cash flows of an individual subsidiary may appear not to support the carrying values of its fixed assets, yet from a group perspective there is no impairment, because the subsidiary is part of a profitable IGU.

8.44 Such situations may be numerous where wholly-owned subsidiaries are concerned and can be illustrated by reference to the examples in the standard that discuss how IGUs are identified. For example, a low-return supporting route operated by a transport group may reside in a separate subsidiary company, yet be part of an IGU that includes a profitable trunk route that is fed by the supporting route. Another example is where a factory owned by a subsidiary company is operating with surplus capacity, but the IGU comprises this and a number of other sites (owned by other subsidiary companies) at which the product can be made – overall there is no impairment, because demand is such that there is not enough surplus capacity to close any one site.

8.45 Transfer pricing also creates difficulties. A subsidiary may be only breaking even because it sells its output to a fellow subsidiary at cost, yet they are part of the same IGU from a group perspective. Where subsidiaries are separate IGUs, one subsidiary may be unprofitable, because it sells output to a fellow subsidiary at below-market prices. Conversely, the transferee subsidiary might be profitable, because it buys goods and services from its fellow subsidiary at below-market prices. The standard indicates (from a group's perspective) that the cash inflows of the transferor IGU and the cash outflows of the transferee IGU that are used in the value in use calculations should be adjusted to reflect market prices rather than internal transfer prices. Consequently, where there is an impairment in the consolidated financial statements the situation could arise where the assets of the 'profitable' subsidiary, rather than those of the 'unprofitable' subsidiary, might be impaired after such adjustments have been made to their respective cash flow forecasts.

8.46 In situations such as those outlined above, it cannot automatically be assumed that the allocation of impairment losses in subsidiaries' own financial statements would follow the way they are allocated in the consolidated financial statements. This is because FRS 11 has to be applied individually to all financial statements that are intended to give a true and fair view of a reporting entity's financial position and profit or loss. Therefore, in general, if the recoverable amount of an asset to a subsidiary (that is, the present value of the future cash flows obtainable by the subsidiary) does not support its carrying value, it should be treated as impaired in the subsidiary's financial statements. However, where wholly-owned subsidiaries enter into transactions at transfer prices that differ significantly from market prices (and such market prices are freely available), it does not make much sense to treat an asset as being impaired in a subsidiary if the carrying value in the subsidiary is supported when its cash flows are re-based to external market prices. In cases where a subsidiary is not earning an economic return on its assets in terms of its separate cash flows, the absence of any impairment loss should require explanation in the subsidiary's financial statements in order to give a true and fair view.

Recognition of impairment losses

Chapter 9

Reversals of impairment losses

General rules

9.1 FRS 11 requires impairment losses recognised in previous periods to be reversed in certain circumstances where the recoverable amount of the assets concerned subsequently increases. This corresponds to the requirement in the Companies Act that where a company has made provision for a diminution in value, but the factors that gave rise to it no longer apply to any extent, then the company must write back the provision to that extent. [4 Sch 19(3)].

9.2 For tangible fixed assets and investments in subsidiaries, associates and joint ventures, the reversal of an impairment loss should be recognised where the recoverable amount increases *"because of a change in economic conditions or in the expected use of the asset"*. [FRS 11 para 56]. This rule is based on the premise that the original impairment is caused by the inability of the asset to generate sufficient returns to recover its carrying amount. Once there is a change in economic conditions or in the expected use of the asset that enables the asset to recover its former carrying amount, the reason for the impairment ceases to apply. For intangible assets and goodwill the criteria for reversing impairment losses are stricter than for other assets (see para 9.13 below).

9.3 The amount of any reversal that can be recognised is restricted to increasing the carrying value of the relevant assets to the carrying value that would have been recognised had the original impairment not occurred (that is, after taking account of normal depreciation that would have been charged had no impairment occurred). [FRS 11 para 56]. In respect of depreciable assets, therefore, any reversals of impairment losses will tend not to be as large as the original impairment loss.

9.4   Indicators that impairment losses may have reversed are the reverse of those that indicated the impairment loss in the first place. Companies should consider whether there have been favourable events or changes in circumstances since the impairment loss was recognised that would indicate that the impairment loss no longer exists or may have decreased. If there are indicators, the recoverable amount of the relevant assets or IGUs should be estimated again. Such changes include situations where the recoverable amount increases as a result of further capital investment or a reorganisation, the benefits of which had been excluded from the original measurement of value in use (see chapter 7 for examples showing how the recognition and reversal rules operate in respect of future reorganisation and capital investment).

9.5   It should be borne in mind that this exercise would only be undertaken if there is evidence of a significant improvement in actual performance or future prospects that would give rise to a material reversal of an impairment loss. As with the original impairment calculations, amounts recognised in respect of reversals are likely to be broad estimates; in fact, it could be positively misleading in terms of reporting performance to have regular impairment losses and reversals resulting from imputing spurious accuracy into the calculations.

9.6   The standard explains that increases in value in use should not be recognised as reversals of impairment losses if they arise simply from:

- The passage of time, resulting from the unwinding of the discount rate that was applied to arrive at the present value of expected future cash flows.

- The occurrence of forecast cash outflows – once the forecast cash outflows have happened they are no longer part of the value in use calculation and the value in use, therefore, increases.

[FRS 11 para 58].

9.7 The reason why the two events described in the previous paragraph do not give rise to the reversal of an impairment loss is because, whilst the value in use admittedly increases, the underlying reasons for the original impairment have not been removed. All that has happened is that time has passed and the expected cash flows have occurred – the service potential of the asset has not increased. The effect is illustrated in the following example:

Example

An asset cost £100 on 1 January 20X0. Its expected useful life is 5 years; depreciation is on a straight-line basis. An impairment review is carried out as at 31 December 20X0 when the carrying value is £80. The projected cash flows are as follows:

	20X1	20X2	20X3	20X4
Cash flows (nominal total 82; present value 64)	13	22	23	24

Using a discount rate of 10%, the present value of the cash flows (value in use) at 31 December 20X0 is £64. Thus an impairment loss of £16 is recognised.

The impaired carrying value of £64 is then depreciated on a straight-line basis over the remaining 4 years of its expected useful life. Assuming the cash flows materialise as projected in the impairment calculation, the carrying value and value in use (present value of remaining cash flows discounted at 10%) at each year end are as follows:

	20X0	20X1	20X2	20X3	20X4
Carrying value	64	48	32	16	-
Value in use	64	57	41	22	-

It can be seen that the value in use at 31 December 20X1, 20X2 and 20X3 exceeds the carrying amount. The reason is a combination of the unwinding of the discount (as the future cash flows get nearer, their present value increases)

117

and the fact that the cash flows themselves increase during the life of the asset. But there is no reversal of the original impairment loss.

The profit and loss accounts for the remaining life of the asset are as follows (ignoring any timing differences between cash flows and profit):

	20X1	20X2	20X3	20X4
Profit before depreciation	13	22	23	24
Depreciation	(16)	(16)	(16)	(16)
Profit (loss) before interest	(3)	6	7	8

The effect of discounting is that a profit before interest of £18 emerges over the remaining 4 years' life of the asset. Discounting the cash flows in the first place reduced the value in use from the nominal amount of £82 to a present value of £64. The corollary of this is that the discount of £18 unwinds over those 4 years, in effect leaving an operating profit to cover the cost of capital. Of course, this profit does not accrue in any even pattern, because (a) the cash flows themselves are uneven and (b) depreciation is on an arbitrary straight-line basis.

9.8　It should be noted, however, that where a reversal of an impairment loss is recognised because economic conditions have changed, the FRS does not suggest that any increase in value in use that is due to 'the passage of time' should be estimated as a separate component and excluded from the reversal. In most practical situations this would be quite unrealistic.

9.9　To illustrate accounting for reversals, consider the following example:

Example

The history of a company's fixed assets is as follows:

	Investment in subsidiary £'000	Tangible fixed assets £'000
Cost at 1 January 20X1	10	6
Value at 31 December 20X1	8	5
Value at 31 December 20X2	* 5	* 3
Value at 31 December 20X3	9	4

* only these decreases in value are impairments. All other diminutions in value have arisen from a general fall in prices.

Ignoring the normal depreciation rules for the purposes of this example (and assuming historical cost rules apply), FRS 11 and the Companies Act apply as follows:

■ At 31 December 20X1 both the investment and the fixed asset have fallen in value, but this is due solely to a general fall in prices. It is determined, following an impairment review that the recoverable amount of the investment and the fixed asset remain at £10,000 and £6,000 respectively. In these circumstances, the directors *could* (if they wish) write down the amount of the investment in subsidiary to £8,000. (This is because the Act permits, but does not require, provision to be made for the diminution in value of a fixed asset *investment* that the directors consider to be only temporary). However, the directors could not write down the value of the tangible fixed asset to £5,000 under the historical cost rules. (This is because the Act allows tangible fixed assets to be written down in value only in circumstances where the diminution in value is expected to be *permanent*. Also, in terms of FRS 11, there has been no impairment of the fixed asset.)

■ At 31 December 20X2 a change in economic circumstances has occurred which leads the directors to believe that the recoverable amounts of the investment and the fixed asset have fallen to £5,000 and £3,000 respectively. Accordingly, the directors must write down the amount of the investment in subsidiary to £5,000 (whether or not they wrote it down to £8,000 at 31 December 20X1). In addition, they *must* write down the value of the tangible fixed asset to £3,000. This is because the fall in value of each of them is expected to be *permanent* and because in terms of FRS 11 there has been an impairment loss.

■ At 31 December 20X3, due to a further change in economic circumstances the recoverable amounts have been restored to £9,000 and £4,000 respectively and the reasons for the original impairment have disappeared. Therefore, the directors must write back £4,000 in respect of the investment in subsidiary and £1,000 in respect of the tangible fixed asset. This is because the reasons that gave rise to the provision for diminution in value/impairment loss on each of them have ceased to apply to that extent. Had the increase in the recoverable amount occurred only because of the passage of time (unwinding of discount) or because forecast cash outflows had occurred, the impairment losses could not be written back, because the reasons for the original impairment would not have ceased to apply.

9.10   Accounting for the reversal of an impairment loss should be consistent with the treatment adopted when the impairment was recognised. Where the asset is held at historical cost, the reversal should be recognised in the current year's profit and loss account, since the original loss would have been charged in the profit and loss account.

9.11   For a revalued asset, the reversal of an impairment loss should be recognised in the profit and loss account to the extent that the original impairment loss (adjusted for subsequent depreciation) was recognised in the profit and loss account. Any remaining balance of the reversal of an impairment loss should be recognised in the statement of total recognised gains and losses, since part of the original impairment loss would have been charged there. [FRS 11 para 66].

9.12 The reversal calculations for revalued assets can be rather complex, as illustrated in the following example.

Example – recognition and reversal of impairment loss on revalued asset

At 31 December X1 an asset was purchased for 100. Its expected useful economic life is 20 years. Three years later it was revalued to 136.

At 31 December X6 the asset was reviewed for impairment and written down to its recoverable amount of 50.

The following table shows the movements in the asset's book value on a depreciated historical cost basis and as actually recognised in the financial statements.

	Depreciated historical cost	Revalued carrying value
31 December X1 – cost	100	100
Depreciation (3 years)	(15)	(15)
Revaluation	–	51
31 December X4	85	136
Depreciation (2 years)	(10)	(16)
31 December X6	75	120
Impairment loss	(25)	(70)
31 December X6 after impairment loss	50	50

The impairment loss of 70 at 31 December X6 is not caused by a clear consumption of economic benefits, and so the loss is charged in the statement of total recognised gains and losses until the carrying amount reaches depreciated historical cost and thereafter in the profit and loss account, as follows:

Statement of total recognised gains and losses	45
Profit and loss account	25
Impairment loss	70

At 31 December X8 economic conditions have improved and the asset's recoverable amount is estimated to be 90.

If no impairment loss had been recognised, the carrying value at 31 December 1998 would have been 104 (120 at 31 December X6 less 2 years of further depreciation of 16), which is greater than the recoverable amount of 90. Therefore, the whole of the increase in the carrying value can be treated as a reversal of the previous impairment loss. It should be noted that if the carrying value had been increased to more than 104, the excess would be treated as a revaluation, not a reversal of the impairment. [FRS 11 para 59].

The impairment loss should be reversed, as indicated in the following table.

	Depreciated historical cost		Carrying value
	Before impairment	After impairment	
31 December X6	75	50	50
Depreciation (2 years)	(10)	(7)	(7)
31 December X8	65	43	43
Reversal of impairment loss	-	22	47
31 December 98 after reversal	65	65	90

The reversal of the impairment loss of 47 is recognised as follows:

Profit and loss account	22
Statement of total recognised gains and losses	25

The profit and loss account figure of 22 represents the amount of the original impairment loss that was charged in the profit and loss account of 25 less an adjustment for the additional depreciation that would have been charged had the asset been carried at depreciated historical cost of 3. The balance of the reversal of 25 is credited in the statement of total recognised gains and losses.

Special rules for goodwill and intangible assets

9.13 Impairment losses relating to capitalised goodwill and intangible assets may be reversed only in limited circumstances. These are where (a) an external event caused the original impairment loss, and (b) subsequent external events clearly and demonstrably reverse the effects of that event in a way that was not foreseen in the original impairment calculations. [FRS 11 para 60]. FRS 11 makes an exception to this rule for intangible assets with a readily ascertainable market value, where impairment losses may be reversed to the extent that the net realisable value (based on market value) subsequently increases to above the impaired carrying value. [FRS 11 para 60]. However, there are very few intangible assets in that category.

9.14 For goodwill, the objective of restricting reversals of impairment losses is to prevent a goodwill write-off from being credited back to the profit and loss account if the credit is in effect attributable to the generation of new non-purchased goodwill. The accounting rules generally for goodwill and intangible assets are similar. Consequently, situations that justify reversals are likely to be rare and in most cases amounts written off goodwill or intangible assets will stay written off. The reason given for the different approaches to tangible and intangible assets is that tangible fixed assets can in any case be revalued, whereas goodwill and most intangible assets cannot.

9.15 An example of a situation that would meet the reversal criteria for an intangible asset is as follows.

Example

A brand name had previously been written off because a product had been withdrawn from the market as a result of a health scare that raised concerns about its safety. The safety concerns subsequently prove to be unfounded and the health authorities approved the product's reintroduction. The company's management had assumed that the product's withdrawal would be permanent when they recognised the impairment loss.

In this example, the impairment loss was caused by an external event (the health scare). An external event (the removal of the safety concerns and the permission to reintroduce the product to the market) clearly and demonstrably has reversed the effects of the external event that caused the impairment loss in a way that was not foreseen in the original impairment calculations. Consequently, the impairment loss should be reversed to the extent that the brand's recoverable amount has increased above its current written down value (assuming that the brand regains some value after the health scare).

9.16   An example of originating and reversing external events that would meet the reversal criteria for goodwill is the introduction of a new law that damages profitability (resulting in a goodwill write-off) and that is subsequently repealed by a new government. Another example is the confiscation of assets in an overseas territory (resulting in a goodwill write-off) that are subsequently released to allow the business to continue its operations. In both of these examples the original goodwill has been reclaimed.

9.17   The recoverable amount of an acquired business may increase in subsequent years after an impairment loss has been recognised, but the improvement will often be unrelated to the circumstances that gave rise to the original impairment. One example is where goodwill has been written off because a competitor has introduced a better product to the market; some years later, the company launches a new product of its own and develops a different market. Another example is where a business has been reorganised to curtail underperforming operations, resulting in a write-off of goodwill; in later years, the business may expand again as new market opportunities arise. In neither of these examples would the turnaround justify reversing the impairment loss relating to the goodwill even though the recoverable amount of the business has increased above the balance sheet value of its net assets and goodwill. This is because the higher value of goodwill that now exists includes goodwill that has been generated internally since the original impairment.

9.18 If, however, the reason for an impairment write-down was a competitor coming into the market and a reversal of the impairment was attributable to the competitor subsequently withdrawing from the market (or modifying its pricing policy in a way that was not foreseen), the criteria for recognising the reversal of the impairment loss in respect of goodwill would be met.

9.19 It should be noted that if the net assets of a business included impaired carrying values for both purchased goodwill and tangible fixed assets, the situation may occur where some impairment loss reversals are permitted (for tangible fixed assets) and others are not (for goodwill and most intangible fixed assets). This situation may occur with business restructurings. Goodwill and tangible fixed assets of businesses in need of reorganisation may have to be written down (there is a concession, though, for recent acquisitions – see chapter 7); if their values are restored as a result of reorganisation, only the impairment losses relating to the tangible fixed assets may be written back.

9.20 The amount that can be written back to reverse an impairment loss is restricted to an amount that increases the carrying value of the goodwill or intangible asset to the carrying value that would have been recognised had the original impairment not occurred (that is, after taking account of normal depreciation that would have been charged had the impairment not occurred). [FRS 11 para 61].

Reversals of impairment losses

Chapter 10

Presentation and disclosures

Presentation of impairment losses in performance statements

Assets carried at historical cost

10.1   FRS 11 requires impairment losses recognised in the profit and loss account to be included within operating profit under the appropriate statutory heading, and disclosed as an exceptional item if appropriate. [FRS 11 para 67]. This applies to goodwill as well as fixed assets.

10.2   The formats in Schedule 4 to the Act prescribe the headings under which depreciation and other amounts written off tangible and intangible fixed assets are to be included in the profit and loss account. Under Format 1, where expenses are classified by function, an impairment loss would generally be charged under the same format heading as depreciation of (or other amounts written off) the relevant assets. Under Format 2, where expenses are classified by type, there is a separate heading 'depreciation and amounts written off tangible and intangible fixed assets'.

Revalued assets

10.3   For revalued assets, FRS 11 introduces rules for recognition of impairment that are more conservative than the Act's requirements in respect of temporary diminutions in value.

10.4   Although FRS 11 does not use the term 'temporary diminutions in value' it distinguishes two types of impairments. These are impairments arising from:

- A clear consumption of economic benefits.
- Other impairments of revalued fixed assets.

10.5   The FRS requires that the former of these two types of impairment should be recognised in the profit and loss account in its entirety, because it is similar to depreciation. No part of it should be taken to the statement of total recognised gains and losses. [FRS 11 para 63]. Examples of clear consumption of economic benefits are physical damage, contamination, obsolescence, deterioration in quality of service – often something wrong with the asset itself.

10.6   Other impairments are accounted for by recognising them in the statement of total recognised gains and losses, until the carrying amount reaches depreciated historical cost. Thereafter, the balance of the impairment is recognised in the profit and loss account. [FRS 11 para 63].

10.7   This category is intended to cover impairments caused by a general fall in prices, for example a general slump in the property market. However, the FRS recognises that in many cases it will be unclear whether an impairment loss is the result of a consumption of economic benefits or some other cause – for example, when there is a fall in demand for an asset's output or services. The development appendix explains that where there is doubt whether the impairment is caused by a reduction in the quantum of an asset's service potential, it should be treated as falling into the other category, that is, the loss is recognised in the statement of total recognised gains and losses, until the carrying amount reaches depreciated historical cost. [FRS 11 App IV para 20].

10.8   An asset's recoverable amount may be reduced by specific factors that do not necessarily affect the general market, say, the establishment of a local competitor to a retail store. Whereas, there may be no physical impairment of the asset, there may be evidence that the impairment has not been caused by a general fall in prices and thus it could be argued that the impairment has been caused by a reduction in its service potential. But rarely will such situations be clear cut.

10.9 The FRS appears to acknowledge that a downward revaluation of a previously revalued asset may constitute partly an impairment due to consumption of economic benefits and partly an impairment due to general price changes. It may be difficult, in practice, to determine whether or not this is the case. The prudent approach taken by the standard, however, makes this less of an issue, because the standard requires all impairments of an asset below depreciated historical cost to be taken to the profit and loss account. (Note, however, that the standard does not apply to investment properties).

10.10 Impairment losses recognised in the profit and loss account should be included in operating profit under the appropriate statutory heading and disclosed as exceptional if appropriate. Impairment losses recognised in the statement of total recognised gains and losses should be disclosed separately on the face of that statement. [FRS 11 para 67].

10.11 It should be noted that if a company's policy is to carry assets at market value and market value is below recoverable amount, the shortfall is not an impairment under FRS 11. The additional write-down would be recognised in the statement of total recognised gains and losses as a revaluation deficit.

10.12 Where, therefore, the revaluation of a fixed asset results in a revalued amount that is below the previous carrying value and is below the value in use of that asset, FRS 11 only requires the asset to be written down, if necessary, to the value in use figure. The difference between the value in use figure and the (lower) revalued amount is simply a valuation adjustment which is then shown in the statement of total recognised gains and losses.

Example

A tangible fixed asset cost £100 and is subject to a revaluation policy to reflect its current market value. Its previous revalued carrying amount was £150, with the surplus of £50 taken to the statement of total recognised gains and losses and the revaluation reserve.

In the current year the fixed asset is revalued and the revalued amount is £80 (in this example, for simplicity, depreciation has been ignored).

An impairment review is done on the asset and the recoverable amount (higher of net realisable value and value in use) is determined to be £90.

The following describes how the revaluation deficit of £70 (£150 – £80) should be accounted for:

(a)   If the impairment of £60, that is, the difference between carrying value of £150 and recoverable amount of £90, is considered to have arisen due to a clear consumption of economic benefits, it should be charged in its entirety to the profit and loss account and shown under the appropriate statutory heading in arriving at operating profit.

The previous revaluation surplus of £50 in the revaluation reserve may then be transferred through reserves (but not through the statement of total recognised gains and losses) to profit and loss reserve.

(b)   If the impairment of £60 is considered not to have arisen from a clear consumption of economic benefits, it should be charged as to £50 to the statement of total recognised gains and losses and £10 to the profit and loss account, again under the appropriate heading in arriving at operating profit. The charge of £50 to the statement of total recognised gains and losses should be shown on the face of that statement.

(c)   In both cases, that is whether the impairment loss is due to a clear consumption of economic benefits or not, the remaining revaluation adjustment of £10 to reduce the asset from its recoverable amount of £90 to its revalued amount of £80 is shown in the statement of total recognised gains and losses. This is because it corresponds to a temporary diminution under the Companies Act rules and such diminutions should be taken, via the statement of total recognised gains and losses, to the revaluation reserve.

10.13   In the above example, a diminution in value of £10 below cost was charged in the statement of total recognised gains and losses rather than the profit and loss account, because that amount was purely a market value adjustment and not an impairment. Consider the presentation in the following year if a further impairment is identified.

Example

The facts are as in the previous example. In the following year the fixed asset's market value has fallen from £80 to £50. A further impairment review is carried out and the recoverable amount is estimated also to be £50 (that is, it has fallen from £90 to £50).

The impairment loss in the following year is £40 (£90 less £50). However, the loss to be recognised in the year (in the profit and loss account) is only £30, because a loss of £10 was charged in the previous year (in the statement of total recognised gains and losses) as a revaluation deficit. In effect that revaluation deficit of £10 has become an impairment loss. But, in accordance with FRS 3, as the loss of £10 has already been recognised in the statement of total recognised gains and losses (albeit not as an impairment loss), it is not shown again in the profit and loss account. Instead, that part of the impairment loss would be charged to profit and loss account reserve by means of a reserve transfer in the reserves note (that is, crediting revaluation reserve and debiting profit and loss account reserve by £10).

Assets held for disposal

Loss on disposal or impairment loss?

10.14   FRS 3 requires losses on disposals of fixed assets or operations (including provisions in respect of them) to be charged after operating profit and before interest. [FRS 3 para 20]. FRS 11 requires impairment losses recognised in the profit and loss account to be charged in operating profit under the appropriate statutory heading. [FRS 11 para 67]. If FRS 11 was interpreted in isolation, most losses recognised in connection with asset disposals would be impairments (charged against operating profit) rather than losses on disposals (non-operating exceptional items).

That is because in most cases any previously unidentified shortfall between an asset's carrying value and its recoverable amount that is identified as a result of a decision to sell or terminate would be an impairment, not a loss on disposal.

10.15   The apparent conflict may be interpreted as follows when the requirements of FRS 3 and FRS 11 are considered together. Impairment losses in respect of fixed assets and businesses that are to be retained must be charged in arriving at operating profit. Impairment losses that, in FRS 3 terms, are provisions for losses on disposals (that is, they are recognised as a result of a decision to dispose of the assets or business concerned) should be shown under the relevant one of the three headings in paragraph 20 of FRS 3. In the latter case, if the disposal has not occurred before the balance sheet date, the company would be expected to provide evidence that the asset or operation would not be retained. For example, the asset or business would probably be being actively marketed and it would be reasonable to expect that the disposal would be completed before the next interim accounts and in any event before the end of the next financial year.

10.16   This apparent inconsistency between FRS 3 and FRS 11 gives rise to some anomalies. If an asset is put up for sale and has not previously been reviewed for impairment, the loss on sale is presented in accordance with paragraph 20 of FRS 3. If, however, an impairment loss is identified earlier as a result of carrying out an impairment review in circumstances required by FRS 11, the loss would be presented as part of operating profit in accordance with FRS 11.

10.17   A similar issue arises where a company undertakes a fundamental reorganisation having a material effect on the nature and focus of its operations. FRS 3 requires the costs incurred to be shown after operating profit under a separate caption. Costs incurred often involve write-offs of assets and goodwill, which are regarded as impairments under FRS 11, as well as other reorganisation costs. In such circumstances, it is logical to present all the costs of the fundamental reorganisation, including the impairments, under the relevant FRS 3 caption.

Disposal of previously impaired asset

10.18　Where a previously impaired fixed asset is sold and the proceeds exceed the impaired carrying value, the gain should be recognised in the profit and loss account. A question arises whether the whole of the gain should be shown under the heading 'profits or losses on the disposal of fixed assets' (after operating profit) or whether at least part of the gain should be recognised as a reversal of the past impairment and be included in operating profit.

10.19　Paragraph 21 of FRS 3 requires the profit on disposal to be accounted for in the profit and loss account of the period in which the disposal occurs as the difference between the net sale proceeds and the net carrying amount, whether carried at historical cost (less any provisions made) or at a valuation. Therefore, the whole of the gain should be shown after operating profit (except where the gain is in effect no more than a marginal adjustment to depreciation previously charged).

10.20　However, where a previously impaired fixed asset has increased in value and has not been disposed of by the year end, paragraph 56 of FRS 11 requires the asset's carrying value to be increased if its recoverable amount has increased because of a change in economic conditions or in the expected use of the asset. The reversal of an impairment loss should be recognised in the profit and loss account to the extent that (a) the original impairment loss was charged in the profit and loss account and (b) the reversal increases the carrying amount up to the amount that it would have been had the original impairment not occurred. It is logical that the reversal of the impairment loss should be credited under the same statutory heading that the original impairment loss was charged, that is, included within operating profit.

Other financial statement disclosures

Fixed asset movements

10.21 In the notes showing fixed asset movements, impairment losses should be disclosed as follows:

■ For assets held at historical cost, the impairment loss should be included within the cumulative depreciation. The cost of the asset should not be reduced.

■ For revalued assets held at market value (that is, existing use value or open-market value) the impairment loss should be included within the revalued carrying amount and not shown within any cumulative depreciation.

■ For revalued assets held at depreciated replacement cost, an impairment loss charged to the profit and loss account should be included within cumulative depreciation. The revalued carrying amount of the asset should not be reduced. An impairment loss charged to the statement of total recognised gains and losses should be deducted from the revalued carrying amount of the asset.

[FRS 11 para 68].

10.22 FRS 10, which applies to goodwill and intangible assets and FRS 15, which applies to tangible fixed assets, are rather more specific on detailing the movements. They require impairment losses, and reversals of past impairment losses, to be disclosed separately in the note that reconciles the movements between the opening and closing balances for goodwill and each class of intangible and tangible asset. [FRS 10 para 53; FRS 15 para 100].

Revalued assets held at market value

10.23   For revalued assets held at market value, revaluations are usually reflected in the reconciliation of fixed asset movements by adjusting the gross revalued carrying amount (that is, before depreciation) to the new market value. Accumulated depreciation charged up to the date of the new valuation is eliminated from the reconciliation. The disclosure of impairment losses in the reconciliation does not distinguish between impairments that are caused by a consumption of economic benefits (charged to the profit and loss account) and other impairments that are deemed to result from general changes in prices (charged to the statement of total recognised gains and losses). All impairments are deducted from the gross revalued carrying amount before depreciation and, hence, none are shown within accumulated depreciation.

10.24   The treatment of revalued assets held at market value is illustrated in the following example. It shows that all impairment losses are in effect treated as downward valuations in the reconciliation of fixed asset movements.

Example

An asset cost £200 and has a useful life of 20 years; it is depreciated on a straight-line basis. At the end of year 3 it was revalued to £220 (compared with depreciated historical cost of £170).

At the end of year 5, the asset had a carrying value of £194 (comprising the revalued amount of £220 less accumulated depreciation of £26 relating to years 4 and 5). On a depreciated historical cost basis, the carrying value would have been £150 (comprising cost of £200 less accumulated depreciation of £50 relating to years 1 to 5).

At the end of year 5, as a result of an impairment review of the IGU to which the asset contributes, the recoverable amount of the IGU is found to be lower than its carrying value. The allocation of the impairment loss in accordance with paragraphs 48 and 49 of FRS 11 results in the asset being written down to its net realisable value (which is based on its current market value). The disclosure of the impairment loss in the reconciliation of fixed asset movements is illustrated in three different scenarios:

A   Recoverable amount is £150. The impairment loss of £44 (which is equal to the surplus of the revalued carrying value of £194 over the depreciated historical cost of £150) is charged in the statement of total recognised gains and losses (that is, treated as a downward revaluation) because the loss is not considered to have been caused by a consumption of economic benefits .

B   Recoverable amount is £150. The impairment loss of £44 is considered to have been caused by a consumption of economic benefits and is charged in the profit and loss account.

C   Recoverable amount is £100. The impairment loss of £94 is charged £44 as in A above in the statement of total recognised gains and losses (that is, the surplus of the revalued carrying value of £194 over the depreciated historical cost of £150) and £50 (the balance) in the profit and loss account.

Impairment loss

	A	B	C
Carrying value	194	194	194
Recoverable amount	150	150	100
Impairment loss	44	44	94
Charged:			
STRGL	44	–	44
Profit and loss account	–	44	50
Total	44	44	94

The impairment losses would be disclosed in the reconciliation of fixed asset movements as follows:

Note of fixed asset movements			
	A	**B**	**C**
Valuation			
At 1 January 05	220	220	220
Impairment	(44)	(44)	(94)
Valuation adjustment	(26)	(26)	(26)
At 31 December 05	150	150	100
Accumulated depreciation			
At 1 January 05	13	13	13
Charge for the year	13	13	13
Valuation adjustment	(26)	(26)	(26)
At 31 December 05	–	–	–
Net book value			
At 31 December 04	207	207	207
At 31 December 05	150	150	100

It should be noted that the valuation adjustment of £26 shown as movements under the 'valuation' and 'accumulated depreciation' headings is necessary to eliminate accumulated depreciation from the reconciliation; thus the recoverable amount at 31 December 05 is treated as a new valuation.

Revalued assets held at depreciated replacement cost

10.25 The treatment of revalued fixed assets carried at market value may be contrasted with the treatment of revalued fixed assets carried at depreciated replacement cost, where impairment losses charged in the profit and loss account should be included within accumulated depreciation. If the revalued asset in the previous example had been valued at depreciated replacement cost, the treatment in the reconciliation of fixed movements would be different, as illustrated in the following example.

Example

The facts are the same as in the previous example, except that the asset was revalued at depreciated replacement cost at the end of year 3. FRS 15 states that both the cost or revalued amount and the accumulated depreciation at the date of revaluation may be restated, so that the carrying amount of the asset after revaluation equals its revalued amount. [FRS 15 para 101]. If this approach was adopted, the valuation of £220 (net replacement cost) would be 'grossed up' to disclose a gross replacement cost and, separately, accumulated depreciation to reflect the portion of the asset's useful life already consumed, as follows:

Cost or valuation	£
Cost b/f	200
Revaluation	59
Gross replacement cost	259
Accumulated depreciation	
B/f	30
Revaluation	9
	39
Net replacement cost	220

The impairment at the end of year 5 would be shown as follows, under each of the three scenarios set out in the previous example.

Note of fixed asset movements			
	A	**B**	**C**
Gross replacement cost			
At 1 January 05	259	259	259
Impairment loss	(44)	–	(44)
At 31 December 05	215	259	215
Accumulated depreciation			
At 1 January 05	52	52	52
Charge for the year	13	13	13
Impairment loss	–	44	50
At 31 December 05	65	109	115
Net book value			
At 31 December 04	207	207	207
At 31 December 05	150	150	100

The impairment losses shown in the above reconciliation can be identified directly with the amounts charged in the profit and loss account (shown under accumulated depreciation) and in the statement of total recognised gains and losses (shown under gross replacement cost).

Value in use calculations

10.26 Where an impairment loss is recognised and has been measured by reference to value in use, the discount rate applied to the cash flows should be disclosed. If a risk-free discount rate is used, some indication of the risk adjustments made to the cash flows should be given. [FRS 11 para 69].

10.27 Where, in measuring value in use, the period before a steady or declining growth rate is assumed extends to more than five years, the financial statements should disclose the length of the longer period and the circumstances justifying it. [FRS 11 para 72].

10.28   Where, in measuring value in use, the long-term growth rate used has exceeded the long-term average growth rate for the country or countries in which the business operates, the financial statements should disclose the growth rate assumed and the circumstances justifying it. [FRS 11 para 73].

10.29   It should be noted that the disclosures referred to in the previous two paragraphs are not limited to circumstances where an impairment loss has actually been recognised. Thus, if a formal impairment review has been carried out and no impairment loss has been recognised, some disclosure of the facts appears to be necessary if the normal constraints on the growth assumptions relating to long-term cash flow forecasts have been exceeded when measuring value in use.

10.30   For the five years following each impairment review, where recoverable amount has been based on value in use, the cash flows achieved should be compared with those forecast. If the cash flows achieved show that an impairment loss should have been recognised in previous periods, that loss should be recognised in the current period, unless it has already reversed. Where an impairment loss would have been recognised in a previous period had forecasts of future cash flows been more accurate, but the impairment has since reversed and the reversal is permitted to be recognised by FRS 11, the impairment now identified and its subsequent reversal should be disclosed. [FRS 11 para 71].

Reversals

10.31   Where a previously recognised impairment loss has been reversed, the reasons for the reversal should be disclosed, including any changes in the assumptions upon which calculation of recoverable amount is based. [FRS 11 para 70].

Companies Act disclosures

10.32   The Companies Act requires that where a company has made any provision for diminution in value, or has written back any provision for diminution in value, it must disclose the amounts involved (either in the profit and loss account or in the notes to the financial statements). [4 Sch 19]. The amounts to be disclosed are:

■   Provisions made in respect of the permanent diminution in value of fixed assets (impairment losses recognised under FRS 11 would normally be regarded as permanent). [4 Sch 19(2)].

■   Provisions made in respect of the temporary diminution in value of fixed asset investments. [4 Sch 19(1)].

■   Amounts written back to the extent that the circumstances that gave rise to the provisions no longer apply. [4 Sch 19(3)].

10.33   The amounts disclosed must be split between the three headings, but amounts that fall within the same heading may be aggregated. [4 Sch 19].

Presentation and disclosures

Chapter 11

Comparison with Iass

11.1   The IASC rules on impairment are to be found in IAS 36, 'Impairment of assets', issued in July 1998. The principles for identifying and measuring impairment losses are similar to those in FRS 11. Both standards require that the recoverable amount of an asset should be estimated whenever there is an indication that the asset might be impaired and that an impairment loss should be recognised if the asset's carrying value exceeds its recoverable amount.

11.2   IAS 36's definition of recoverable amount is equivalent to that in FRS 11 – the higher of an asset's net selling price (equivalent to net realisable value) and its value in use. As in FRS 11, impairment reviews are often carried out for groups of assets, which are referred to as 'cash-generating units' (equivalent to FRS 11's 'income-generating units' and similarly defined).

11.3   The detailed requirements in IAS 36 and FRS 11 for carrying out impairment reviews are also broadly similar. The principal differences are:

- Where an acquired business is merged with an existing business, IAS 36 does not require any value to be attributed to internally generated goodwill in the existing business for the purpose of establishing a carrying value of the cash-generating unit that is compared with its value in use. The effect of this difference is that some impairment losses relating to purchased goodwill that are recognised under the FRS 11 methodology will escape recognition under IAS 36. (However, unlike FRS 10, IAS 22 does not allow an indefinite useful life to be assigned to purchased goodwill and so there will always be an amortisation charge for goodwill under IAS.)

■ IAS 36 has no equivalent to the 'look-back' test in FRS 11 that requires the accuracy of value in use estimates used in impairment reviews to be reviewed (and, if necessary, reworked) for the next five years.

■ IAS 36 does not give any special attention to the costs and benefits of reorganisation and capital expenditure relating to newly acquired businesses, whereas FRS 11 makes an exception and allows them to be taken into account in the calculation of value in use. However, there may be little difference in practice, since IAS 22 permits certain post-acquisition restructuring costs to be recognised as provisions as part of the fair value exercise, whereas FRS 7 does not.

11.4 The other principal differences are:

■ For previously revalued assets, to the extent that there is a revaluation surplus, IAS 36 requires impairment losses to be charged to the revaluation surplus and any excess should be charged to the income statement. FRS 11 requires impairments caused by a consumption of economic benefits to be charged in full to the profit and loss account, even if there is a revaluation surplus on the asset concerned.

■ Under IAS 36, the treatment of intangible assets for the purpose of allocating impairment losses and the recognition of reversals of impairment losses is aligned with that relating to tangible assets; FRS 11 is more conservative by treating intangible assets similarly to purchased goodwill.

■ FRS 11 and IAS 36 both have similar rules that control the longer-term growth rates that may be assumed in the value in use calculations. FRS 11 requires disclosure if the guidelines have been exceeded, whereas IAS 36 does not.

Comparison with IASs

Appendix

FRS 11 Impairment of Fixed Assets and Goodwill

Financial Reporting Standard 11 is set out in paragraphs 1-82.

The Statement of Standard Accounting Practice, which comprises the paragraphs set in bold type, should be read in the context of the Objective as stated in paragraph 1 and the definitions set out in paragraph 2 and also of the Foreword to Accounting Standards and the Statement of Principles for Financial Reporting currently in issue.

The explanatory paragraphs contained in the FRS shall be regarded as part of the Statement of Standard Accounting Practice insofar as they assist in interpreting that statement.

Appendix IV 'The development of the FRS' reviews considerations and arguments that were thought significant by members of the Board in reaching the conclusions on the FRS.

© *The Accounting Standards Board*

Appendix

CONTENTS

149

ADOPTION OF FRS 11 BY THE BOARD

APPENDICES

I   DETERMINING PRE-TAX DISCOUNT RATES

II   NOTE ON LEGAL REQUIREMENTS

III COMPLIANCE WITH INTERNATIONAL ACCOUNTING STANDARDS

IV THE DEVELOPMENT OF THE FRS

SUMMARY

a Financial Reporting Standard 11 'Impairment of Fixed Assets and Goodwill' sets out the principles and methodology for accounting for impairments of fixed assets and goodwill. Investments covered by the Accounting Standards Board's project on derivatives and other financial instruments are excluded from the scope of the FRS. Also excluded are investment properties, which are being considered further in the light of other Board projects and the international project on investment properties.

b It would be unnecessarily onerous for all fixed assets and goodwill to be tested for impairment every year. In general, fixed assets and goodwill need be reviewed for impairment only if there is some indication that impairment has occurred. (Requirements for additional impairment reviews of goodwill and intangible assets in certain circumstances are included in FRS 10 'Goodwill and Intangible Assets'.)

c Where possible, individual fixed assets should be tested for impairment. However, impairment can often be tested only for groups of assets because the cash flows upon which the calculation is based do not arise from the use of a single asset. In these cases, impairment is measured for the smallest group of assets (the income-generating unit) that produces a largely independent income stream, subject to constraints of practicality and materiality.

d Impairment is measured by comparing the carrying value of the fixed asset or income-generating unit with its recoverable amount. The recoverable amount is the higher of the amounts that can be obtained from selling the fixed asset or income-generating unit (net realisable value) or using the fixed asset or income-generating unit (value in use).

e   Net realisable value is the expected proceeds of selling the fixed asset or income-generating unit less any direct selling costs. Value in use is calculated by discounting the expected cash flows arising from the use of the fixed asset or assets in the income-generating unit at the rate of return that the market would expect from an equally risky investment.

f   In some cases a detailed calculation of value in use will not be necessary. A simple estimate may be sufficient to demonstrate that either value in use is higher than carrying value, in which case there is no impairment, or value in use is lower than net realisable value, in which case impairment is measured by reference to net realisable value.

g   If an acquisition that gives rise to goodwill is merged with an existing business, the requirements of the FRS necessitate the calculation of the amount of any internally generated goodwill in the existing business at the date of the merger because that amount will need to be used in the calculation of any subsequent impairment loss in the merged business.

h   The reversal of past impairment losses is recognised when the recoverable amount of a tangible fixed asset or investment in a subsidiary, an associate or a joint venture has increased because of a change in economic conditions or in the expected use of the asset. Increases in the recoverable amount of goodwill and intangible assets are recognised only when an external event caused the recognition of the impairment loss in previous periods, and subsequent external events clearly and demonstrably reverse the effects of that event in a way that was not foreseen in the original impairment calculations.

i   Impairment losses are recognised in the profit and loss account, unless they arise on a previously revalued fixed asset. Impairment losses on revalued fixed assets are recognised in the statement of total recognised gains and losses until the carrying value of the asset falls below depreciated historical cost unless the impairment is clearly caused by a consumption of economic benefits, in which case the loss is recognised in the profit and loss account. Impairments below depreciated historical cost are recognised in the profit and loss account.

FINANCIAL REPORTING STANDARD 11

Objective

1 The objective of this FRS is to ensure that:

    (a) fixed assets and goodwill are recorded in the financial statements at no more than their recoverable amount;

    (b) any resulting impairment loss is measured and recognised on a consistent basis; and

    (c) sufficient information is disclosed in the financial statements to enable users to understand the impact of the impairment on the financial position and performance of the reporting entity.

Definitions

2 The following definitions shall apply in the FRS and in particular in the Statement of Standard Accounting Practice set out **in bold type**.

Impairment:-

A reduction in the recoverable amount of a fixed asset or goodwill below its carrying amount.

Income-generating unit:-

A group of assets, liabilities and associated goodwill that generates income that is largely independent of the reporting entity's other income streams. The assets and liabilities include those directly involved in generating the income and an appropriate portion of those used to generate more than one income stream.

Intangible assets:-

Non-financial fixed assets that do not have physical substance but are identifiable and controlled by the entity through custody or legal rights.

Net realisable value:-

The amount at which an asset could be disposed of, less any direct selling costs.

Purchased goodwill:-

The difference between the cost of an acquired entity and the aggregate of the fair values of that entity's identifiable assets and liabilities.

Readily ascertainable market value:-

In relation to an intangible asset, the value that is established by reference to a market where:

(a) the asset belongs to a homogeneous population of assets that are equivalent in all material respects; and

(b) an active market, evidenced by frequent transactions, exists for that population of assets.

Recoverable amount:-

The higher of net realisable value and value in use.
Tangible fixed assets:-

Assets that have physical substance and are held for use in the production or supply of goods or services, for rental to others, or for administrative purposes on a continuing basis in the reporting entity's activities.

Value in use:-

The present value of the future cash flows obtainable as a result of an asset's continued use, including those resulting from its ultimate disposal.

Scope

3 The FRS applies to all financial statements that are intended to give a true and fair view of a reporting entity's financial position and profit or loss (or income and expenditure) for a period.

4 Reporting entities applying the Financial Reporting Standard for Smaller Entities (FRSSE) are exempt from the FRS unless preparing consolidated financial statements, in which case they should apply the FRS to such statements as required by the FRSSE.*

5 The requirements of the FRS apply to purchased goodwill that is recognised in the balance sheet and all fixed assets, except:

(a) fixed assets within the scope of the FRS addressing disclosures of derivatives and other financial instruments;

---

* *Reporting entities applying the FRSSE are generally exempt from applying this FRS. However, if they prepare consolidated financial statements, the FRSSE in force at the date of the publication of this FRS requires them to apply SSAP 22 to purchased goodwill arising on consolidation. It is envisaged that a future revision of the FRSSE will require smaller entities adopting the FRSSE and preparing consolidated financial statements to replace that reference to SSAP 22 with an equivalent reference to FRS 10 and this FRS.*

(b) investment properties as defined in SSAP 19 'Accounting for investment properties';

(c) an entity's own shares held by an ESOP and shown as a fixed asset in the entity's balance sheet under UITF Abstract 13 'Accounting for ESOP Trusts'; and

(d) costs capitalised pending determination (ie costs capitalised while a field is still being appraised) under the Oil Industry Accounting Committee's SORP 'Accounting for oil and gas exploration and development activities'.

6   Many investments are covered by the Accounting Standards Board's project on derivatives and other financial instruments and hence are excluded from this FRS. However, investments in subsidiary undertakings, associates and joint ventures are excluded from the scope of that project and are, therefore, included within the scope of this FRS.

7   The FRS does not apply to purchased goodwill that was written off to reserves under SSAP 22 'Accounting for goodwill' and has not been recognised on the balance sheet under FRS 10 'Goodwill and Intangible Assets'.

Indications of impairment

8   A review for impairment of a fixed asset or goodwill should be carried out if events or changes in circumstances indicate that the carrying amount of the fixed asset or goodwill may not be recoverable.

9   Impairment occurs because something has happened either to the fixed assets themselves or to the economic environment in which the fixed assets are operated. It is possible, therefore, to rely on the use

of indicators of impairment to determine when a review for impairment is needed.

10 Examples of events and changes in circumstances that indicate an impairment may have occurred include:

■   a current period operating loss in the business in which the fixed asset or goodwill is involved or net cash outflow from the operating activities of that business, combined with either past operating losses or net cash outflows from such operating activities or an expectation of continuing operating losses or net cash outflows from such operating activities

■   a significant decline in a fixed asset's market value during the period

■   evidence of obsolescence or physical damage to the fixed asset

■   a significant adverse change in:

   — either the business or the market in which the fixed asset or goodwill is involved, such as the entrance of a major competitor

   — the statutory or other regulatory environment in which the business operates

   — any 'indicator of value' (for example turnover) used to measure the fair value of a fixed asset on acquisition

■   a commitment by management to undertake a significant reorganisation

■   a major loss of key employees

■ a significant increase in market interest rates or other market rates of return that are likely to affect materially the fixed asset's recoverable amount.

11 The above indicators of impairment will trigger an impairment review only if they are relevant to the measurement of goodwill or fixed assets. For example, short-term market interest rates may increase without affecting the rate of return the market would require on long-term assets, with the result that there is no effect on the recoverable amount of such assets. Such increases in short-term rates would not trigger an impairment review.

12 If any such events or changes in circumstances are identified, a review of the useful economic lives and residual values of the fixed assets or goodwill affected is appropriate: even if the fixed assets or goodwill are not impaired, their remaining useful economic lives and residual values may have changed as a result of the events or changes in circumstances.

13 The requirements of this FRS are such that if no such events or changes in circumstances are identified, and there are no other indications that a tangible fixed asset or investment in a subsidiary, associate or joint venture has become impaired, there is no requirement for an impairment review. For tangible fixed assets, impairments will therefore be a relatively infrequent addition to depreciation. Additional requirements to perform impairment reviews for goodwill and intangible assets that are amortised over periods of more than 20 years or not at all are set out in FRS 10 'Goodwill and Intangible Assets'.

Recognition and measurement of impairment losses

14 The impairment review should comprise a comparison of the carrying amount of the fixed asset or goodwill with its recoverable amount (the higher of net realisable value and value in use). To the

extent that the carrying amount exceeds the recoverable amount, the fixed asset or goodwill is impaired and should be written down. The impairment loss should be recognised in the profit and loss account unless it arises on a previously revalued fixed asset, in which case it should be recognised as required by paragraph 63.

15 If either net realisable value or value in use is higher than the carrying amount of a fixed asset or goodwill, the fixed asset or goodwill is not impaired and there is no need to calculate the other amount.

16 If no reliable estimate of net realisable value can be made, the recoverable amount is determined by value in use alone.

17 If net realisable value is lower than the carrying amount of the fixed asset, before writing down the asset to net realisable value it is necessary to establish whether value in use is higher. If it is, the recoverable amount will be based on value in use, not net realisable value.

18 Requirements and guidance relating to the calculation of net realisable value and value in use are set out in paragraphs 22 – 46 below. In many cases, a detailed calculation of value in use will not be necessary because a simple estimate will be sufficient to demonstrate that value in use is either above carrying value, in which case there is no impairment, or is below net realisable value, in which case the recoverable amount will not be based on value in use.

19 In determining whether recoverable amount should be based on value in use or net realisable value, the deferred tax balances that would arise in each case need to be taken into account. For example, if net realisable value is £100 and would give rise to a deferred tax liability of £30 and value in use is £110 and would give rise to a deferred tax liability of £45, recoverable amount is based on net realisable value.

20 If a fixed asset is not held for the purpose of generating cash flows either by itself or in conjunction with other assets, for example certain fixed assets held for charitable purposes, it is not appropriate to measure the asset at an amount based on expected future cash flows. In such cases it may not be appropriate to write down the fixed asset to its recoverable amount – an alternative measure of its service potential may be more relevant.

21 When an impairment loss on a fixed asset or goodwill is recognised, the remaining useful economic life and residual value should be reviewed and revised if necessary. The revised carrying amount should be depreciated over the revised estimate of the remaining useful economic life.

Calculation of net realisable value

22 The net realisable value of an asset that is traded on an active market will be based on market value.

23 Net realisable value is defined as the amount at which an asset could be disposed of, less any direct selling costs. Examples of direct selling costs are legal costs and stamp duty. Any costs relating to the removal of a sitting tenant are also direct selling costs of a building. However, costs associated with reducing or reorganising the business rather than selling the fixed asset, such as redundancy costs incurred when a factory is sold, are not direct selling costs.

Calculation of value in use

24 The value in use of a fixed asset should be estimated individually where reasonably practicable. Where it is not reasonably practicable to identify cash flows arising from an individual fixed asset, value in use should be calculated at the level of income-generating units. The carrying amount of each income-generating unit containing the fixed asset or goodwill under review should be

compared with the higher of the value in use and the net realisable value (if it can be measured reliably) of the unit.

25 The value in use of a fixed asset is the present value of the future cash flows obtainable as a result of the asset's continued use, including those resulting from its ultimate disposal. In practice, it is not normally possible to estimate the value in use of an individual fixed asset: it is the utilisation of groups of assets and liabilities, together with their associated goodwill, that generates cash flows. Hence value in use will usually have to be estimated in total for groups of assets and liabilities. These groups are referred to as income-generating units.

26 Because it is necessary to identify only material impairments, in some cases it may be acceptable to consider a group of income-generating units together rather than on an individual basis.

Income-generating units

27 Income-generating units should be identified by dividing the total income of the entity into as many largely independent income streams as is reasonably practicable. Except as permitted by paragraph 32, each of the identifiable assets and liabilities of the entity, excluding deferred tax balances, interest-bearing debt, dividends payable and other items relating wholly to financing, should be attributed to (or apportioned between) one (or more) income-generating unit(s).

28 To perform impairment reviews as accurately as possible:

■ the groups of assets and liabilities that are considered together should be as small as is reasonably practicable, but

- the income stream underlying the future cash flows of one group should be largely independent of other income streams of the entity and should be capable of being monitored separately.

Income-generating units are therefore identified by dividing the total income of the business into as many largely independent income streams as is reasonably practicable in the light of the information available to management.

29 In general terms, the income streams identified are likely to follow the way in which management monitors and makes decisions about continuing or closing the different lines of business of the entity. Unique intangible assets, such as brands and mastheads, are generally seen to generate income independently of each other and are usually monitored separately. Hence they can often be used to identify income-generating units. Other income streams may be identified by reference to major products or services.

Examples 1-4:
Identification of income-generating units

Example 1
A transport company runs a network comprising trunk routes fed by a number of supporting routes. Decisions about continuing or closing the supporting routes are not based on the returns generated by the routes in isolation but on the contribution made to the returns generated by the trunk routes.

An income-generating unit comprises a trunk route plus the supporting routes associated with it because the cash inflows generated by the trunk routes are not independent of the supporting routes.

Example 2
A manufacturer can produce a product at a number of different sites. Not all the sites are used to full capacity and the manufacturer can choose how much to make at each site. However, there is not enough surplus capacity to enable any one site to be closed. The cash inflows generated by any one site therefore depend on the allocation of production across all sites.

The income-generating unit comprises all the sites at which the product can be made.

Example 3
A restaurant chain has a large number of restaurants across the country. The cash inflows of each restaurant can be individually monitored and sensible allocations of costs to each restaurant can be made.

Each restaurant is an income-generating unit by itself. However, any impairment of individual restaurants is unlikely to be material. A material impairment is likely to occur only when a number of restaurants are affected together by the same economic factors. It may therefore be acceptable to consider groupings of restaurants affected by the same economic factors rather than each individual restaurant.

Example 4
An entity comprises three stages of production, A (growing and felling trees), B (creating parts of wooden furniture) and C (assembling the parts from B into finished goods). The output of A is timber that is partly transferred to B and partly sold in an external market. If A did not exist, B could buy its timber from the market. The output of B has no external market and is transferred to C at an internal transfer price. C sells the finished product in an external market and the sales revenue achieved by C is not affected by the fact that the three stages of production are all performed by the entity (unlike example 1, where the sales revenue of the trunk routes is affected by the existence of supporting routes run by the same entity).

A forms an income-generating unit and its cash inflows should be based on the market price for its output. B and C together form one income-generating unit because there is no market available for the output of B. In calculating the cash outflows of the income-generating unit B+C, the timber received by B from A should be priced by reference to the market, not any internal transfer price.

---

30 Income-generating units are defined by allocating the assets and liabilities of the reporting entity, excluding deferred tax balances, interest-bearing debt, dividends payable and other items relating

wholly to financing, to the identified income streams. Certain assets and liabilities that are directly involved in the production and distribution of individual products may be attributed directly to one unit. Central assets, such as group or regional head offices, and working capital may have to be apportioned across the units on a logical and systematic basis. The resulting income-generating units will be complete and non-overlapping, so that the sum of the carrying amounts of the units equals the carrying amount of the net assets (excluding tax and financing items) of the entity as a whole, as illustrated in examples opposite.

Example 5: Allocation of head office assets to income-generating units

An entity has three independent income streams, A, B and C, with net assets directly involved in the income streams with carrying amounts of £100 million, £ 150 million and £200 million respectively. In addition there are head office net assets with a carrying amount totalling £18 million. The relative proportion of the head office resources used by the income streams is 2:3:4. The income-generating units are defined as follows:

Income-generating unit	A	B	C	Total
Net assets directly attributable to income-generating unit (£ million)	100	150	200	150
Head office net assets (£ million)	4	6	8	18
Total (£ million)	104	156	208	468

If there were an indication that a fixed asset in income-generating unit B was impaired, the recoverable amount of B would be compared with £156 million, not £150 million. Similarly, the cash flows upon which the value in use of B is based would include the relevant portion of any cash outflows arising from central overheads.

31 The income stream of a fixed asset to be disposed of will be largely independent of the income stream of other assets. Such an asset therefore forms an income-generating unit of its own and does not belong to any other income-generating unit.

Central assets

32 **If it is not possible to apportion certain central assets meaningfully across the income-generating units to which they contribute, these assets may be excluded from the individual income-generating units. However, an additional impairment review should be performed on the excluded central assets. In this review, the income-generating units to which the central assets contribute should be combined and their combined carrying amount (including that of the central assets) should be compared with their combined value in use.**

Example 6:
Alternative approach to allocation of head office assets to income-generating units

With this approach, in example 5 above the recoverable amount of B would be compared with £150 million, not £156 million. Then a further impairment test would be required on the whole entity comparing its recoverable amount with the total carrying value of £468 million.

33 If there is any working capital in the balance sheet that will generate cash flows equal to its carrying amount, the carrying amount of the

working capital may be excluded from the income-generating units and the cash flows arising from its realisation/settlement excluded from the value in use calculation.

34 Capitalised goodwill should be attributed to (or apportioned between) income-generating units or groups of similar units. If they were acquired as part of the same investment and are involved in similar parts of the business, individual units identified for the purpose of monitoring the recoverability of assets may be combined with other units to enable the recoverability of the related goodwill to be assessed.

35 Goodwill is allocated to income-generating units in the same way as are the assets and liabilities of the entity. However, where several similar income-generating units are acquired together in one investment, the units may be combined to assess the recoverability of the goodwill. The income-generating units are first reviewed individually for the purposes of assessing the recoverability of any capitalised intangible assets and tangible fixed assets and then, as illustrated in example 7 below, the combined unit is reviewed to assess the recoverability of the goodwill.

> **Example 7: Alternative approach to allocation of goodwill to income-generating units**
>
> An entity acquires a business comprising three income-generating units, A, B and C. After five years, the carrying amount of the net assets in the income-generating units and the purchased goodwill compares with the value in use as follows (there is no reliable estimate of net realisable value for any of the income-generating units or the business as a whole):

Income-generating unit	A	B	C	Goodwill	Total
Carrying amount (£ million)	80	120	140	50	390
Value in use (£ million)	100	140	120		360

An impairment loss of £20 million is recognised in respect of income-generating unit reducing its carrying amount to £120 million and the total carrying amount to £370 million. A further impairment loss of £10 million is then recognised in respect of the goodwill.

Cash flows

36 The expected future cash flows of the income-generating unit, including any allocation of central overheads but excluding cash flows relating to financing and tax, should be based on reasonable and supportable assumptions. The cash flows should be consistent with the most up-to-date budgets and plans that have been formally approved by management. Cash flows for the period beyond that covered by formal budgets and plans should assume a steady or declining growth rate. Only in exceptional circumstances should:

(a) the period before the steady or declining growth rate is assumed extend to more than five years; or

(b) the steady or declining growth rate exceed the long-term average growth rate for the country or countries in which the business operates.*

37 In exceptional circumstances, the use of a long-term growth rate that is higher than the average country growth rate may be Justified. This may, for example, be the case where:

---

* *The UK post-war average growth in gross domestic product, expressed in real terms, is 2.25 per cent (source: Financial Statement and Budget Report March 1998, HM Treasury)*

(a) the long-term growth rate for the relevant industry is expected to be significantly higher than the relevant country growth rate; and

(b) the business under review is expected to grow as rapidly as the industry as a whole, taking into account the likelihood of new competitors entering such an industry.

38 Subject to paragraph 39 below, future cash flows should be estimated for income-generating units or individual fixed assets in their current condition. They should not include:

(a) future cash outflows or related cost savings (for example reductions in staff costs) or benefits that are expected to arise from a future reorganisation for which provision has not yet been made; or

(b) future capital expenditure that will improve or enhance the income-generating units or assets in excess of their originally assessed standard of performance or the related future benefits of this future expenditure.

39 In the case of a newly acquired income-generating unit such as a subsidiary, the purchase price will reflect the synergies and other opportunities for making more effective use of the assets as a result of the acquisition. In some of these cases, in order to obtain the benefits from its investment, it may be necessary for the purchaser to undertake related capital expenditure and reorganisations. Consequently, in assessing the future cash flows of the investment, the costs and benefits of such reorganisations and capital expenditure anticipated at the time of performing impairment reviews up to the end of the first full year after acquisition and consistent with budgets and plans at that time may be taken into account in those and subsequent impairment

reviews, to the extent that the investment or reorganisations are still to be incurred.

40   Failure to undertake capital investment or a reorganisation according to the planned schedule may call into question the validity of continuing to forecast that the investment or reorganisation will be undertaken in the future and may be an indication of impairment as discussed in paragraphs 8-13. The costs and benefits of the investment or reorganisation would then have to be omitted from forecasts performed for subsequent impairment reviews. Additionally, the monitoring of cash flows required by paragraph 54 may indicate that impairment has already occurred.

Discount rate

41   The present value of the income generating unit under review should be calculated by discounting the expected future cash flows of the unit. The discount rate used should be an estimate of the rate that the market would expect on an equally risky investment. It should exclude the effects of any risk for which the cash flows have been adjusted and should be calculated on a pre-tax basis.

42   Estimates of this market rate may be made by a variety of means including reference to:

(a)   the rate implicit in market transactions of similar assets;

(b)   the current weighted average cost of capital (WACC) of a listed company whose cash flows have similar risk profiles to those of the income-generating unit; or

(c)   the WACC for the entity *but only if* adjusted for the particular risks associated with the income-generating unit.

43   If method (c) is used the following matters are of note.

- Where the cash flow forecasts assume a real growth rate that exceeds the long-term average growth rate for more than five years, it is likely that the discount rate will be increased to reflect a higher level of risk.

- The discount rates applied to individual income-generating units will always be estimated such that, were they to be calculated for every unit, the weighted average discount rate would equal the entity's overall WACC.

44 The WACC will be a post-tax rate from the entity's point of view, whereas the required discount rate will be a pre-tax rate. Some of the issues that need to be considered in adjusting from a post-tax rate to a pre-tax rate are discussed in Appendix 1.

45 Using a discount rate equal to the rate of return that the market would expect on an equally risky investment is a method of reflecting the risk associated with the cash flows in the value in use measurement. it is likely that this method will be the easiest method of reflecting risk. However, an acceptable alternative is to adjust the cash flows for risk and to discount them using a risk-free rate (eg a government bond rate). Whichever method of reflecting risk is adopted, care must be taken that the effect of risk is not double-counted by inclusion in both the cash flows and the discount rate.

46 If the cash flows to be discounted are expressed in current prices, a real discount rate will be used. If the cash flows are expressed in expected future prices, a nominal discount rate will be used.

Allocation of impairment losses

47 The carrying amounts of the income-generating units under review should be calculated as the net of the carrying amounts of the assets, liabilities and goodwill allocated to the unit.

48 To the extent that the carrying amount of the income-generating unit exceeds its recoverable amount, the unit is impaired. In the absence of an obvious impairment of specific assets within the unit, the impairment should be allocated:

(a) first, to any goodwill in the unit;

(b) thereafter, to any capitalised intangible asset in the unit; and

(c) finally, to the tangible assets in the unit, on a pro rata or more appropriate basis.

49 In this allocation, which aims to write down the assets with the most subjective valuations first, no intangible asset with a readily ascertainable market value should be written down below its net realisable value. Similarly, no tangible asset with a net realisable value that can be measured reliably should be written down below its net realisable value.

Allocation when acquired businesses are merged with existing operations

50 Where an acquired business is merged with an existing business and results in an income-generating unit that contains both purchased and (unrecognised) internally generated goodwill:

(a) the value of the internally generated goodwill of the existing business at the date of merging the businesses should be estimated and added to the carrying amount of the income-generating unit for the purposes of performing impairment reviews;[*]

---

[*] *The internally generated goodwill will not be recognised in the financial statements.*

   (b) any impairment arising on merging the businesses should be
       allocated solely to the purchased goodwill within the newly
       acquired business;

   (c) subsequent impairments should be allocated pro rata between
       the goodwill of the acquired business and that of the existing
       business;

   (d) the impairment allocated to the existing business should be
       allocated first to the (notional) internally generated goodwill;
       and

   (e) only the impairments allocated to purchased goodwill (and, if
       necessary, to any recognised intangible or tangible assets)
       should be recognised in the financial statements.

51 An acquired business may be merged with an existing operation of the
    reporting entity in such a way that a single income-generating unit
    includes the assets and liabilities of both the acquired and the existing
    businesses. This combined income-generating unit contains both
    acquired and internally generated goodwill and any future impairment
    needs to be apportioned between the two. This can be done by
    notionally adjusting the carrying amount of the income-generating unit
    to recognise a notional carrying amount for the internally generated
    goodwill of the existing operation at the date of merging the two
    businesses.

52 The notional carrying amount of the internally generated goodwill is
    estimated by deducting the fair values of the net assets and purchased
    goodwill within the existing income-generating unit from its estimated
    value in use before combining the businesses. This calculation will
    need to be done whenever an acquisition that gives rise to goodwill is
    merged with an existing business. The notional balance is assumed to
    be subject to the same pattern of amortisation as is applied to the
    purchased goodwill.

53 Because the comparison with value in use will have resulted in the recognition of any impairment of the existing business at the time of merging it with the acquired business, any initial impairment in the combined income-generating unit will, by definition, relate to the acquired business. Any subsequent impairment cannot be attributed directly to either the acquired or the existing businesses and is therefore apportioned between the notional internally generated goodwill and the purchased goodwill pro rata to their current carrying values.

Example 8: Allocation of impairment losses when an acquired business is merged with existing operations

Assumptions

An entity acquires for £60 million a business having net assets with a total fair value of £40 million, resulting in purchased goodwill of £20 Million. The acquired business is merged with an existing operation that has net assets with a fair value of £100 million and a carrying amount of £70 million. The value in use of the existing operation at the time of the acquisition is £150 million, implying that the existing operation had internally generated goodwill of £50 million.

Five years later, the carrying amount of the net assets of the combined income-generating unit is £105 million and the carrying amount of the purchased goodwill is £10 million (goodwill is being amortised over 10 years). Value in use is £119 million and there is no reliable estimate of net realisable value.

Calculation of impairment loss	£m
Carrying amount of net assets	105
Carrying amount of goodwill	10
Notional carrying amount of internally generated goodwill at the date of acquisition(assuming notional amortisation on same basis as for purchased goodwill)	25
Total	140
Value in use	119
Impairment	21

The impairment is allocated on a pro rata basis (2:5) to the purchased goodwill and internally generated goodwill, resulting in the recognition of an impairment loss of £6 million and purchased goodwill being written down to £4 million.

If value in use were £98 million, the resulting total impairment loss of £42 Million would be allocated first to the goodwill (purchased and notional amount of internally generated) of £35 million, then to any intangible assets, then to the tangible fixed assets in the income-generating unit, resulting in the recognition of an impairment loss of £17 million (write-down of purchased goodwill £10 million, write-down of intangible and tangible assets £7 million).

Subsequent monitoring of cash flows

54 For the five years following each impairment review where the recoverable amount has been based on value in use, the cash flows achieved should be compared with those forecast. If the actual cash flows are so much less than those forecast that use of the actual cash flows could have required recognition of an impairment in previous periods, the original impairment

calculations should be re-performed using the actual cash flows. Any impairment identified should be recognised in the current period unless the impairment has reversed and the reversal of the loss is permitted to be recognised by paragraph 56 or 60 below.

55 In order to check whether an impairment would have arisen, the original calculation is re-performed using the cash flows that have actually occurred but without revising any other cash flows or assumptions (except those that change as a direct consequence of the occurrence of the actual cash flows, eg where a major cash inflow has been delayed for a year). If this recalculation identifies an impairment, the loss should be recognised in the current period. However, the entity may also recalculate value in use using revised assumptions in order to assess the current value in use. If this current value in use shows a reversal of the impairment that would have been recognised had the actual cash flows been used in the original calculation, and that reversal is permitted to be recognised under the FRS, recognition of an impairment loss is not required. Instead, the impairment that would have been recognised and its subsequent reversal are disclosed (paragraph 71).

Reversal of past impairments

Tangible fixed assets and investments in subsidiaries, associates and joint ventures

56 If, after an impairment loss has been recognised, the recoverable amount of a tangible fixed asset or investment increases because of a change in economic conditions or in the expected use of the asset, the resulting reversal of the impairment loss should be recognised in the current period to the extent that it increases the carrying amount of the fixed asset up to the amount that it would have been had the original impairment not occurred. The reversal of the impairment loss should be recognised in the profit and loss

account unless it arises on a previously revalued fixed asset, in which case it should be recognised as required by paragraph 66.

57 Events and circumstances that are the reverse of those set out in paragraph 10 as triggers for an impairment review may indicate that the recoverable amount of a fixed asset has increased. The increase in the recoverable amount must arise from a change in economic conditions or in the expected use of the asset. This would include situations where the recoverable amount increases as a result of further capital investment or a reorganisation, the benefits of which had been excluded from the original measurement of value in use.

58 Increases in value in use may arise simply because of.

(a) the passage of time: as future cash inflows become closer, their discounted value increases. (Where value in use has been calculated using cash flows based on current prices and a real discount rate, value in use may also increase because of the effect of general inflation on current prices.)

(b) the occurrence of forecast cash outflows: once the cash outflows are past, they are no longer part of the value in use calculation and value in use therefore increases.

Such increases in value may not be recognised as reversals of an impairment loss.

59 The recognition of an increase in the recoverable amount of a tangible fixed asset above the amount that its carrying amount would have been had the original impairment not occurred is a revaluation, not a reversal of an impairment.

Goodwill and intangible assets

60 The reversal of an impairment loss on intangible assets and goodwill should be recognised in the current period if, and only if.

(a) an external event caused the recognition of the impairment loss in previous periods, and subsequent external events clearly and demonstrably reverse the effects of that event in a way that was not foreseen in the original impairment calculations; or

(b) the impairment loss arose on an intangible asset with a readily ascertainable market value and the net realisable value based on that market value has increased to above the intangible asset's impaired carrying amount.

61 The reversal of the impairment loss should be recognised to the extent that it increases the carrying amount of the goodwill or intangible asset up to the amount that it would have been had the original impairment not occurred.

62 The recognition of an increase in the recoverable amount of an intangible asset above the amount that its carrying amount would have been had the original impairment not occurred is a revaluation and is addressed by FRS 10 'Goodwill and Intangible Assets'.

Example 9: Allocation and reversal of impairment losses

Assumptions

An income -generating unit comprising a factory, plant and equipment etc and associated purchased goodwill becomes impaired because the product it makes is overtaken by a technologically more advanced model produced by a competitor. The recoverable amount of the income-generating unit falls to £60 million, resulting in an impairment loss of £80 million, allocated as follows:

	Carrying amounts before impairment £m	Carrying amounts after impairment £m
Goodwill	40	–
Patent (with no market value)	20	–
Tangible fixed assets	80	60
Total	140	60

After three years, the entity makes a technological breakthrough of its own, and the recoverable amount of the income-generating unit increases to £90 million. The carrying amount of the tangible fixed assets had the impairment not occurred would have been £70 million.

Calculation of reversal of the impairment loss

The reversal of the impairment loss is recognised to the extent that it increases the carrying amount of the tangible fixed assets to what it would have been had the impairment not taken place, ie a reversal of £10 million of the impairment loss is recognised and the tangible fixed assets written back to £70 million. Reversal of the impairment is not recognised in relation to the goodwill and patent because the effect of the external event that caused the original impairment has not reversed – the original product is still overtaken by a more advanced model.

Revalued fixed assets

63 An impairment loss on a revalued fixed asset should be recognised in the profit and loss account if it is caused by a clear consumption of economic benefits. Other impairments of revalued fixed assets should be recognised in the statement of total recognised gains and losses until the carrying amount of the asset reaches its depreciated historical cost and thereafter in the profit and loss account.

64 An impairment loss arises on a revalued fixed asset whenever the recoverable amount of the asset falls below its carrying amount. In particular, a downward revaluation may comprise, at least in part, an impairment loss. Some of these impairments are caused by a consumption of economic benefits, for example physical damage or a deterioration in the quality of the service provided by the asset, and are operating costs similar to depreciation.

65 Other impairments of revalued fixed assets may result from general changes in prices, for example a general slump in the property market, and are recognised in the statement of total recognised gains and losses as valuation adjustments until the carrying amount of the asset

reaches its depreciated historical cost, and thereafter in the profit and loss account.

66 A reversal of an impairment loss should be recognised in the profit and loss account to the extent that the original impairment loss (adjusted for subsequent depreciation) was recognised in the profit and loss account. Any remaining balance of the reversal of an impairment should be recognised in the statement of total recognised gains and losses.

Presentation and disclosure

67 Impairment losses recognised in the profit and loss account should be included within operating profit under the appropriate statutory heading, and disclosed as an exceptional item if appropriate. Impairment losses recognised in the statement of total recognised gains and losses should be disclosed separately on the face of that statement.

68 In the notes to the financial statements in accounting periods after the impairment, the impairment loss should be treated as follows:

(a) for assets held on a historical cost basis, the impairment loss should be included within cumulative depreciation: the cost of the asset should not be reduced.

(b) for revalued assets held at a market value (eg existing use value or open market value), the impairment loss should be included within the revalued carrying amount.

(c) for revalued assets held at depreciated replacement cost, an impairment loss charged to the profit and loss account should be included within cumulative depreciation: the carrying amount of the asset should not be reduced; an impairment loss charged to the statement of total recognised gains and

losses should be deducted from the carrying amount of the asset.

69 If the impairment loss is measured by reference to value in use of a fixed asset or income-generating unit, the discount rate applied to the cash flows should be disclosed. If a risk-free discount rate is used, some indication of the risk adjustments made to the cash flows should be given.

70 Where an impairment loss recognised in a previous period is reversed in the current period, the financial statements should disclose the reason for the reversal, including any changes in the assumptions upon which the calculation of recoverable amount is based.

71 Where an impairment loss would have been recognised in a previous period had the forecasts of future cash flows been more accurate but the impairment has reversed and the reversal of the loss is permitted to be recognised, the impairment now identified and its subsequent reversal should be disclosed.

72 Where, in the measurement of value in use, the period before a steady or declining long-term growth rate has been assumed extends to more than five years, the financial statements should disclose the length of the longer period and the circumstances justifying it.

73 Where, in the measurement of value in use, the long-term growth rate used has exceeded the long-term average growth rate for the country or countries in which the business operates, the financial statements should disclose the growth rate assumed and the circumstances justifying it.

Date from which effective and transitional arrangements

74 The accounting practices set out in the FRS should be regarded as standard in respect of financial statements relating to accounting periods ending on or after 23 December 1998. Earlier adoption is encouraged but not required.

75 Impairment losses recognised when the standard is implemented for the first time are not the result of a change in accounting policy and should be recognised in accordance with the requirements of the FRS and not as prior period adjustments.

76 The requirement that fixed assets should not be held at more than recoverable amount is a well-established principle. Achieving this objective by applying the method prescribed in the FRS is not a change in accounting policy but is similar to a change in accounting estimate.

Amendment of other accounting standards

77 The FRS supersedes paragraphs 19 and 20 of SSAP 12 'Accounting for depreciation' and the last sentence in paragraph 22 is amended to:

"Depreciation charged before the revaluation should not be written back to the profit and loss account."

78 In the appendix to SSAP 17 'Accounting for post balance sheet events', examples (b) and (c) of adjusting events are amended to:

"(b) *Property:* A valuation that provides evidence of an impairment in value.

(c) *Investments:* The receipt of a copy of the financial statements or other information in respect of an unlisted company that provides evidence of an impairment in the value of a long-term investment."

79 FRS 2 'Accounting for Subsidiary Undertakings' is amended as follows:

(a) the second sentence of paragraph h(i) of the summary becomes

"They are to be included at their carrying amount when the restrictions carne into force, subject to any write-down for impairment, and no further accruals are to be made for profits or losses of those subsidiary undertakings, unless the parent undertaking still exercises significant influence."

(b) the fifth and sixth sentences of paragraph 27 become

"The carrying amount of subsidiary undertakings subject to severe long-term restrictions should be reviewed and written down for any impairment in value. When impairment is assessed, each subsidiary undertaking should be considered individually."

(c) the second sentence of paragraph 28 becomes

"Similarly, any amount previously charged for impairment that needs to be written back as a result of restrictions ceasing should be separately disclosed."

(d) the fifth sentence in paragraph 79(a) becomes

"Because severe long-term restrictions may give rise to impairments, the FRS requires the value of the excluded subsidiary undertaking to be reviewed to assess whether any impairment has occurred."

(e) **the eighth and ninth sentences in paragraph 89 become**

"For example, where such an investment has been written down because it is impaired, the effect of applying the Schedule 4A paragraph 9 method of acquisition accounting would be to increase reserves and create an asset (goodwill). In the rare cases where the Schedule 4A paragraph 9 calculation of goodwill would be misleading, goodwill should be calculated as the sum of goodwill arising from each purchase of an interest in the relevant undertaking adjusted as necessary for any subsequent impairment."

80 **In FRS 3 'Reporting Financial Performance', the last sentence of paragraph 45 is amended to**

"In accordance with normal practice, however, any impairments in asset values should be recorded."

81 **FRS 10 'Goodwill and Intangible Assets' is amended as follows:**

(a) **paragraph 39 becomes**

"Except as permitted in paragraph 40 , impairment reviews should be performed in accordance with the requirements of FRS 11 'Impairment of Fixed Assets and Goodwill'."

(b) **paragraph 40(b) becomes**

"(b) performing a full impairment review in accordance with the requirements of FRS 11 only if the initial review indicates that the post-acquisition performance has failed to meet pre-acquisition expectations or if any other previously unforeseen events or changes in circumstances indicate that the carrying values may not be recoverable."

(c) paragraph 73 is deleted.

82 Paragraph 151 of the Guidance Notes to SSAP 21 'Accounting for leases and hire purchase contracts' refers to a "permanent diminution in value". The Guidance Notes were issued by the former Accounting Standards Committee of the CCAB and were not adopted by the Board. Nonetheless, it would be consistent with the above amendments to SSAPs and FRSs if the second sentence in paragraph 151 were deemed to be amended to

"If the asset has suffered an impairment it should be written down to its recoverable amount."

ADOPTION OF FRS 11 BY THE BOARD

Financial Reporting Standard 11 – 'Impairment of Fixed Assets and Goodwill' was approved for issue by the ten members of the Accounting Standards Board.

Sir David Tweedie	(Chairman)
Allan Cook	(Technical Director)
David Allvey	
Ian Brindle	
Dr John Buchanan	
John Coombe	
Raymond Hinton	
Huw Jones	
Professor Geoffrey Whittington	
Ken Wild	

APPENDIX 1:

DETERMINING PRE–TAX DISCOUNT RATES

1 The discount rate reflects the rate of return required on the assets being reviewed, not the way in which they have been financed. Hence it is not affected by any tax relief available on the cost of financing the asset or by any tax paid by the provider of finance.

2 The required pre-tax rate of return is simply the rate of return that will, after tax has been deducted, give the required post-tax rate of return. Because the tax consequence of different cash flows may be different, the pre-tax rate of return is not always the post-tax rate of return grossed up by a standard rate of tax.

3 The effect of discounting pre-tax cash flows at a pre-tax discount rate should be similar to the effect of discounting post-tax cash flows at a post-tax discount rate.

Example

An asset is required to generate a post-tax return of 14 per cent. If the asset cost £100, and generated all of its cash flows in one year's time, the required post-tax cash flows would be £114.

If tax was charged at 30 per cent, pre-tax cash flows of £120 would be required to generate the required post-tax cash flows of £114:

Appendix

	£	£
Pre-tax flows		120
Tax at 30% of £120	(36)	
Allowance for cost of asset at 30%	30	
		-6
		114

Thus the required pre-tax cash flows would be £120, making the required pre-tax rate of return 20 per cent.

The value assigned to the asset would be £100, whether calculated by discounting pre-tax cash flows (£120) by the pre-tax required rate of return (20 per cent) or by discounting post-tax cash flows (£114) by the post-tax required rate of return (14 per cent).

4   However, when an asset becomes impaired, the relationship between pre-tax and post-tax required rates of return may change. This is because, although future pre-tax cash flows reduce, the amount of future tax relief may not. This is taken into account by providing for deferred tax on any timing differences created by the recognition of the impairment loss, not by making any adjustment to the pre-tax discount rate.

Example

Suppose that in the previous example, £100 had been paid for the asset in the expectation that it would generate pre-tax cash flows of at least £120. However, circumstances then changed and the pre-tax cash flows were expected to halve to £60. The cash flows expected in one year's time would therefore be:

	£	£
Pre-tax cash flows		60
Tax at 30% of £60	(18)	
Allowance for cost of asset	30	
		12
		72

Although the pre-tax cash flows have halved, the post-tax cash flows have not reduced so much. Thus discounting the pre-tax cash flows of £60 by 20 per cent (to give a value of £50) no longer produces the same value for the asset as would be achieved by discounting the post-tax cash flows of £72 by 14 per cent (to give a value of £63).

The difference is not eliminated by making any adjustment to the pre-tax rate of return to reflect the tax status of the asset under review. Rather it is eliminated by providing for deferred tax on the timing difference created by the recognition of the impairment loss:

	£
Impaired carrying value of asset (£60 discounted by 20%)	50
Deferred tax asset (impairment of £50, at 30% discounted by 14%)	13*
Total amount recognised in respect of asset	63

---

* *Under SSAP 15, the deferred tax asset might not be recognised and would not be discounted.*

APPENDIX II:

NOTE ON LEGAL REQUIREMENTS

Great Britain

Impairment losses

1   Paragraph 19(1) of Schedule 4 to the Companies Act 1985 allows provisions for diminutions in value of fixed asset investments to be made and the amount to be included in respect of the fixed asset investment to be reduced accordingly. Any provisions that are not shown in the profit and loss account must be disclosed (either separately or in aggregate) in a note to the accounts.

2   Paragraph 19(2) of Schedule 4 requires provisions for diminution in value to be made in respect of any fixed asset that has diminished in value if the reduction in its value is expected to be permanent. The amount to be included in respect of the asset must be reduced accordingly. Any provisions that are not shown in the profit and loss account must be disclosed (either separately or in aggregate) in a note to the accounts.

3   Clearly it is a matter of judgement whether any diminution in value should be treated as permanent (although there must be reasonable grounds for making such a judgement), as indicated by the requirement, referred to again below, that any provision subsequently found not to be necessary has to be reversed.

4   In addition to references to diminutions in value in the paragraphs noted above, the Act allows for the revaluation downwards of fixed assets dealt with under the alternative accounting rules in paragraph 34 of Schedule 4.

5 The FRS concerns itself with impairment rather than permanent diminutions in value. Nevertheless, the distinction between permanent and temporary diminutions in value is inherently recognised in the FRS. A principle is established that impairments that are clearly due to consumption of economic benefits are charged to the profit and loss account. Any such loss is clearly a permanent loss. Other cases of impairment raise separate considerations.

6 Where a fixed asset is impaired, it will always be the case that both the value in use and the net realisable value will be below the carrying amount. Although this does not inevitably signify a loss that is permanent, it would be prudent in relation to fixed assets held at depreciated historical cost to regard such a loss as permanent and, despite any element of uncertainty, charge it to the profit and loss account. In the case of a revalued fixed asset, it would be reasonable to reflect the uncertainty of the permanence of any impairment by treating it as a reversal of any temporary increase in value previously recognised. Such an impairment would be dealt with through the statement of total recognised gains and losses (ie as a revaluation reserve movement). However, if the impairment results in a carrying value below depreciated historical cost, then, as in a pure historical cost context, it would be prudent and reasonable to treat that part of the impairment as being permanent and charge it to the profit and loss account.

Reversals of impairment losses

7 Paragraph 19(3) of Schedule 4 requires that where the reasons for which a provision was made have ceased to apply to any extent, the provision shall be written back to the extent that it is no longer necessary. Where any amounts written back are not shown in the profit and loss account, they must be disclosed (either separately or in aggregate) in a note to the accounts.

8   The FRS requires that, for tangible fixed assets, a reversal of an impairment loss should be recognised when the recoverable amount of an asset increases because of a change in economic conditions – the reason for the impairment was that the asset was not expected to generate sufficient returns to cover its carrying amount. Once it is expected to do so, the reason for the impairment ceases to apply.

9   The FRS explains that the increase in recoverable amount must arise from a change in economic conditions that results in a revised calculation of the recoverable amount. Increases in value in use may arise simply because of:

(a) the passage of time: as future cash inflows become closer, their discounted value increases; or

(b) the occurrence of forecast cash outflows: once the cash outflows are past, they are no longer part of the value in use calculation and value in use therefore increases.

The Board believes that these increases should not give rise to a write-back of the impairment loss because the reason for which the provision was made has not ceased to apply – all that has happened is that time has passed and the expected cash flows have occurred.

10 The Board has received legal advice that a reversal of an impairment loss on goodwill should be recognised only where an external event caused the recognition of the impairment loss in previous periods and subsequent external events clearly and demonstrably reverse the effects of that event in a way that was not foreseen in the original impairment calculations. The Board believes that, for the reasons set out in Appendix IV 'The development of the FRS', the same criterion should apply to intangible assets (except those that have a readily ascertainable market value).

Northern Ireland and the Republic of Ireland

11 The references to the equivalent statutory requirements in Northern
Ireland and the Republic of Ireland are as follows:

Great Britain	*Northern Ireland*	*Republic of Ireland*
Schedule 4 to the Companies Act 1985:	Schedule 4 to the Companies (Northern Ireland) Order 1986:	The Schedule to the Companies (Amendment) Act 1986:
paragraph 19(1)	paragraph 19(1)	paragraph 7(1)
paragraph 19(2)	paragraph 19(2)	paragraph 7(2)
paragraph 19(3)	paragraph 19(3)	paragraph 7(3)
paragraph 34	paragraph 34	paragraph 22

APPENDIX III:

COMPLIANCE WITH INTERNATIONAL ACCOUNTING STANDARDS

1   The International Accounting Standards Committee approved its accounting standard IAS 36 'Impairment of Assets' in April 1998. The basic approach in the IAS is the same as that in the FRS: impairment is measured by comparing the carrying value of fixed assets and goodwill with the higher of net selling price (equivalent to net realisable value) and value in use. Value in use is calculated by discounting the cash flows expected to be generated from the assets.

2   The detailed requirements of the IAS are also very similar to those of the FRS They differ insofar as:

(a)   the FRS requires impairments of revalued assets that are clearly caused by the consumption of economic benefits to be recognised in the profit and loss account (paragraph 63). In contrast, the IAS requires such impairments to be recognised in the profit and loss account only to the extent that the loss exceeds the balance on the revaluation reserve relating to the assets in question.

(b)   to be consistent with FRS 10 'Goodwill and Intangible Assets', the FRS aligns the treatment of intangible assets with that of goodwill, whereas the IAS treats intangibles as being more similar to tangible fixed assets. This has two consequences:

(i)   the FRS allocates impairment losses in an, income-generating unit first to goodwill, secondly to intangible assets and then to tangible fixed assets (paragraph 48). The IAS allocates impairment losses first to goodwill and then pro rata to intangible and tangible assets; and

(ii) the FRS restricts the recognition of reversals of impairment losses on intangible assets (except those with a readily ascertainable market value) to the same limited circumstances in which reversals of impairments of goodwill are recognised (paragraph 60). The IAS recognises reversals of impairments of intangible assets under the same conditions that apply to reversals of impairments of tangible fixed assets.

(c) the FRS has a general rule that in all but exceptional circumstances, longer-term cash flow projections should assume that within five years a steady or declining growth rate of no more than the relevant country average growth rate is achieved (paragraph 36). It requires disclosure if these assumptions are not made. The IAS has a similar general rule but:

- does not require disclosure if the assumptions are not made

- rather than restricting growth rates to those of the relevant country, restricts them to those of the relevant products, industry or country.

(d) if an acquired business has been merged with existing operations, the FRS requires any subsequent impairment to be allocated between the acquired goodwill and the goodwill in the existing operations at the time of merging the two businesses (paragraph 50). The IAS does not include this requirement.

(e) the FRS requires the accuracy of previous estimates of value in use to be monitored for five years following an impairment review (paragraph 54). Any impairment that should have been recognised at the time must be recognised in the current period unless it has since reversed, in which case its non-recognition in past years should be disclosed. The IAS does not include these requirements.

(f) The IAS requires the amounts recognised as impairment losses and reversals of impairment losses to be disclosed in more detail than does the FRS.

3   The rationale for including in the FRS each of the requirements mentioned above is addressed in Appendix IV 'The development of the FRS'.

APPENDIX IV:

THE DEVELOPMENT OF THE FRS

The need for a standard

1   It is accepted practice that a fixed asset should not be carried in financial. statements at more than its recoverable amount, ie the higher of the amount for which it could be sold and the amount recoverable from its future use. However, there is little guidance on how recoverable amount should be measured and when impairment losses should be recognised. As a result, practice is inconsistent and perhaps some impairments may not be recognised on a timely basis.

2   The need for a standard on impairment is increased by the requirement in FRS 10 'Goodwill and Intangible Assets' that, where goodwill and intangible assets have a useful life in excess of twenty years (including those exceptional cases where the life is indefinite), the recoverable amount of the goodwill and intangible assets should be reviewed every year.

3   This FRS sets out a method for measuring and recognising impairment. In developing the FRS the Board has considered comments on its initial proposals that were set out in the Discussion Paper 'Impairment of Tangible Fixed Assets', on the related proposals on impairment set out in FRED 12 'Goodwill and Intangible Assets' and on FRED 15 'Impairment of Fixed Assets and Goodwill'.

Indications of impairment

4   Systematic depreciation ensures that the carrying amount of a fixed asset is reduced to reflect over its useful economic life any reduction in the asset's recoverable amount arising from consumption of economic benefits. A tangible fixed asset that is depreciated in an

appropriate manner is unlikely to become materially impaired unless events or changes in circumstances cause a sudden reduction in the estimate of the recoverable amount. Thus, where tangible fixed assets are depreciated, a requirement for an impairment review to be performed each period would be unnecessary and unduly onerous. The Board believes that, in such circumstances, impairment reviews are necessary only if events or changes in circumstances indicate that the carrying amount may not be recoverable. The additional occasions when impairment reviews are required for intangible assets and goodwill are set out and explained in FRS 10.

Measurement of impairment

Measurement by reference to recoverable amount

5   The FRS requires impairment to be measured by comparing the carrying amount of a fixed asset or income-generating unit with its recoverable amount. The recoverable amount is based on the cash flows that can be generated by the fixed asset or income-generating unit either by sale (net realisable value) or by continued use (value in use). When fixed assets or goodwill are written down to the higher of the amount that can be recovered through sale or continued use, they are recorded at their greatest value to the entity. If the entity chooses not to use or sell the fixed asset or income-generating unit so as to recover the greatest value possible, the loss from not doing so is properly recorded in the period in which the fixed asset or income-generating unit is sold when more could be recovered through use, or in the period(s) in which it is used when more could be recovered through sale.

6   The Board believes that this presents a faithful representation of the economic decisions that are made when a fixed asset or income-generating unit becomes impaired.

7   An alternative approach would be to measure impairment by reference to fair value, being the amount at which an asset or liability could be exchanged in an arm's length transaction between informed and willing parties, other than in a forced or liquidation sale. This is the approach adopted by the US standard FAS 121 'Accounting for the Impairment of Long-Lived Assets and for Long-Lived Assets to Be Disposed Of'. For many assets with a deep active market, fair value, net realisable value and value in use will not be materially different. Where there is no such market or where the entity uses the asset for a specific purpose not generally open to other participants in the market, there may well be a difference between net realisable value and value in use, and the notion of fair value is less well defined. It might, for example, be assumed that fair value is equal to net realisable value (subject to transaction costs) even if value in use is higher, but such an assumption does not reflect the fact that a wining seller would not dispose of the asset for much less than its value in use. Exactly what is the 'fair value' of the asset is open to question.

8   The Board believes that defining recoverable amount as the higher of net realisable value and value in use gives a more precise and clearer indication of the amount to which the asset should be written down and therefore prefers this terminology to the use of the term 'fair value'.

Constraints on estimates of value in use – growth rates and subsequent monitoring

9   The forecasts of future cash flows used to measure the value in use of a business are inevitably subjective. The FRS contains two key controls designed to reduce the risk of over-optimistic forecasting. First, it requires the longer-term projections of cash flows to assume a growth rate that does not normally exceed the long-term average growth rate for the country in which the business operates (paragraph 36). It allows higher rates to be used in the shorter-term forecasts, but

states that only in exceptional (and disclosed) circumstances should these shorter-term forecasts extend beyond five years.

10 The Board recognises that, even in the longer term, growth rates in certain industries will exceed average growth rates for the country as a whole. However, it takes the view that this does not necessarily mean that individual businesses within such industries will grow as quickly: in the longer term, high growth industries may attract new businesses, reducing the opportunities for high growth rates in existing businesses. Hence, where an entity believes that it could justify using an industry growth rate for more than five years, it must disclose what it has done.

11 The second constraint placed on estimates of future cash flows is the requirement to monitor the accuracy of cash flow forecasts for the five years following an impairment review: any impairment that should have been recognised at the time must be recognised in the current period unless it has since reversed, in which case its non-recognition in past years should be disclosed. The aim of the disclosure requirement is primarily to ensure that cash flows are reliable: a record of continually falling short of forecast cash flows will tend to cast doubt on the reliability of current estimates; and awareness that this would have to be disclosed will be an incentive to management to build its forecasts on realistic assumptions.

12 The Board views these two controls as important checks on the reliability of forecasts. They were proposed early on in the development of the FRS and included within the proposals in both the Discussion Paper and the subsequent FRED. They were accepted by most respondents.

Discounting

13 Discounting is a method of reflecting the time value of money and the effect of risk in the valuation of a stream of future cash flows. All

rational economic decisions and, hence, all arm's length transactions reflect the time value of money and the effect of risk. Given that the Board's definition of recoverable amount is based on the economic decisions made when an impairment occurs, value in use must also reflect these factors. If not, value in use would not be measured on a consistent basis with net realisable value and cost (both of which are based on observable transactions and, hence, reflect the time value of money and the effect of risk). A comparison between carrying amount (based on cost), net realisable value and value in use would be meaningless.

14 The Board therefore believes that the cash flows on which value in use is based should either be discounted at a risk-adjusted rate, ie the rate of return that the market would expect on an equally risky investment, or should themselves be adjusted for risk before being discounted at a risk-free rate.

Tax

15 FRED 15 proposed that impairments should be measured on a post-tax basis and the tax element split out for presentation in the financial statements. An alternative approach, adopted by the FASB in FAS 121 and by IASC in IAS 36 'Impairment of Assets', is for value in use to be calculated by discounting the pre-tax cash flows at a pre-tax rate and any further tax consequences recognised by applying a tax standard. The reason behind the approach in FRED 15 was that it discounted the effect of any future capital allowances still to be received, whereas the present tax standard, SSAP 15, does not.

16 A slight majority of respondents to FRED 15 preferred the pre-tax approach, primarily because it was thought to be easier to apply. Given this view and the desirability of harmonisation with the USA and IASC, the Board has decided to change to a pre-tax approach. The question of discounting deferred tax assets and liabilities will be considered as part of the Board's project on deferred tax.

Measurement of impairment when acquired businesses are merged with existing operations

17 The FRS includes specific requirements regarding the measurement of an impairment arising after a purchased business has been merged with existing operations. It requires that any subsequent impairment of the combined business is allocated on a pro-rata basis between the (unrecognised) goodwill in the existing operations and the acquired goodwill. Had this requirement not been included, the effect would be that any impairment of the acquired goodwill would not be recognised unless, and to the extent that, the impairment of the combined business exceeded the value of the unrecognised goodwill at the time of merging.

18 IAS 36 does not include this requirement. Although IASC acknowledged that the requirement would be necessary to measure impairment accurately, it took the view that it would be a difficult requirement to apply in practice. The Board considered this argument, but retained the requirement in the FRS on the grounds that:

■ without the requirement, impairment losses would be understated in the circumstances where the requirement applied.

■ the absence of such a requirement would create an opportunity to avoid the recognition of impairment losses by treating an acquired business as having been merged with a large existing business.

■ the requirement will not have to be applied universally: it will have to be applied only when performing an impairment review of purchased goodwill where the acquired business was merged with an existing business and the goodwill has become partly, but not wholly, impaired. Especially where goodwill is being amortised, these circumstances may not arise often.

Impairment of revalued fixed assets

19 The Board believes that, in principle, impairments of revalued fixed assets fall into two general groups – those that are clearly caused by a consumption of economic benefits and those caused by a general fall in prices. The first type is similar to depreciation and is treated as such, whereas the second type is more like a valuation adjustment that would fall to be recognised in the statement of total recognised gains and losses.

20 However, in many cases it is difficult to allocate an impairment to one or other group with certainty. In order to provide objectivity in the treatment of impairments of revalued fixed assets, the FRS requires that where there is doubt whether the impairment is caused by a reduction in the quantum of the service potential, the impairment loss should be recognised in the statement of total recognised gains and losses until the carrying amount of the asset reaches its depreciated historical cost. Any further impairment should be recognised in the profit and loss account.

21 Although this split between the statement of total recognised gains and losses and the profit and loss account where the type of impairment is unclear is necessarily arbitrary, it has the advantage of being consistent with IAS 16 (revised 1993) 'Property, Plant and Equipment' and IAS 36. It is also likely to be perceived as an equitable approach that does not penalise entitles that revalue their fixed assets.

Reversal of past impairment losses

22 Companies legislation requires provisions for diminutions in value to be written back if the reasons for the provision have ceased to apply. The Board agrees with this principle but is aware that in some cases it will be difficult to distinguish between increases in the value of a fixed asset or income-generating unit that arise because the reasons

for the impairment have ceased to apply and increases in value that arise for some other reason.

23 For tangible fixed assets and investments the Board believes it is acceptable for any increase in value that reverses a previous impairment to be recognised, as long as it results from changed economic conditions or the expected use of the asset and not simply the passage of time or the occurrence of forecast cash flows. After all, increases in value arising from changed economic conditions could be recognised by revaluing the assets.

24 In relation to intangible assets that cannot be revalued and goodwill, the Board does not wish to recognise increases in value attributable to the internal generation of intangible asset value or goodwill. Accordingly, the FRS allows recognition of reversals of past impairments of intangible assets and goodwill only where the increase in value can be clearly attributed to the unexpected reversal of an external event that caused the original impairment to be recognised.

Changes made to FRED 15

25 In the light of comments made by those responding to FRED 15, a number of changes have been made to its proposals. The most significant changes are that:

- investment properties are exempted from the requirements of the FRS. The treatment of investment properties is being considered further in the light of other Board projects and the international project on investment properties. The Board believes that, until this work is complete, it is appropriate to maintain the status quo as set out in SSAP 19 'Accounting for investment properties'.

- an entity's own shares held in an ESOP and shown as a fixed asset in the balance sheet under UITF Abstract 13 'Accounting for ESOP Trusts' are also exempt from the requirements of the

FRS. The Board believes that an entity's own shares should be treated in a manner consistent with other investments, rather than as fixed assets. They will, therefore, be considered as part of the financial instruments project.

■ the FRS requires a pre-tax rather than a post-tax approach to measuring impairment (see paragraphs 15 and 16 above).

■ examples to clarify the principles underlying the identification of income-generating units have been added.

■ an alternative to allocating central assets across income-generating units is allowed – the central assets may instead be tested for impairment by reviewing the combination of all the income-generating units to which they contribute.

■ a requirement has been added (paragraph 38 of the FRS) that value in use should reflect the asset or income-generating unit as it exists at the balance sheet date and hence that In general the costs and benefits of future investment should not be included in the value in use calculation.

■ explanation has been added regarding the circumstances in which the reversal of past impairment losses may be recognised.

Appendix

Index

Public houses, income-generating units (IGUs), 34
Public transport franchises,
income-generating units (IGUs), 31-2
Purchased goodwill,
aggregation, 40, 92, 93-5, 98-9
allocation, 41-5, 92, 93, 96-8
amortisation, 1, 5-6, 14, 18-19, 105, 106
asset-based methods, 43
carrying values, 6, 10
different business units, 42
earnings-based methods, 43
FAS 121: 42
first year review, 19-20
FRS 10: 43, 68, 105, 106
groups of companies, 40
impairment losses, 91-5
impairment reviews, 6, 14, 18-20, 92
income-generating units (IGUs), 39-45
integration of acquired
  businesses, 101-6
positive/negative, 43, 44
price-earnings ratios, 43
reversals, 123-5
sale of business, 41-3
two-tier review, 92, 99-101
US GAAP, 42
useful economic life, 18-19, 42, 68, 105
written off to reserves, 10, 105-6

Recoverable amounts,
company legislation, 1, 5
deferred tax balances, 13-14
definition, 23
impairment reviews, 11-12
income-generating units (IGUs), 30
market value, 129
measurement, 10, 23-8
net realisable value, 11, 23-5
SSAP 12: 5
value in use, 11, 23-4, 25, 26-8

Reorganisations,
cash flow, 56-62
FRS 7: 68
FRS 12: 57
future reorganisations, 58-62
no provision for costs, 60-2
provision for costs, 60
Retailing, income-generating units (IGUs), 31, 32-3
Revaluation,
consumption of economic benefits, 129
market value, 129-31, 135-7
value in use, 129
Reversals,
carrying values, 115
disclosure, 140
fixed assets, 115
impairment losses, 115-25
indicators, 116
intangible assets, 123-5
profit and loss, 120-3
purchased goodwill, 123-5
value in use, 116-17

Sale of assets,
FRS 3: 107-8, 110, 131-3
FRS 12: 107-8, 110
impairment losses, 106-10, 131-3
loss on disposal, 131-3
previously impaired asset, 133
realisable value *see* Net realisable value
subsidiaries, 108-9
Sale of business,
impairment losses, 107
purchased goodwill, 41-3
SORP 2: 9
SSAP 12,
carrying values, 5
recoverable amounts, 5
SSAP 15, deferred tax, 13, 72, 81-2, 85, 87
SSAP 19, investment properties, 9